Wee Bobby Cruickshank

Wee Bobby Cruickshank

The Luckiest Unlucky Golfer in the Game

DIANA SMITH

Alpharetta, GA

ISBN: 978-1-63183-762-3 - Paperback
eISBN: 978-1-63183-763-0 - ePub
eISBN: 978-1-63183-764-7 - mobi

Printed in the United States of America   0 3 2 4 2 0

⊗This paper meets the requirements of ANSI/NISO Z39.48-1992 (Permanence of Paper)

To my husband, Joel,
my critique group, who learned more about golf
than they ever wanted to know,
and Carol, my friend and editor.

Contents

Preface   ix

The Two Bobbys: Jones and Cruickshank   1

Young Bobby   6

The War Years: 1914–1918   10

After the War   18

On His Way: 1924   25

The Beginning of the Golden Journey   32

1926 and the Ten-Inch Putt   35

Travel: Touring in the Twenties and Thirties   40

The Best Year: 1927   48

1928–1930 and the Big Bet   54

Dire Times for Golf: 1931–1932   61

1933–1937: Winding Down   65

Afterword   71

Golf Record   73

Bobby's Rules of Life   75

Bibliography   77

Preface

Before the idea of a professional golf tour, before the time when earning a living as a professional tournament player was a feasible and honorable profession, and before the Masters existed, a group of golfers needing some way to earn a living in the winter months began to plant the seed of what we see today. My grandfather, Wee Bobby Cruickshank, was one of these old-time golfers. Migrating from Scotland with his wife and baby after four-plus years fighting in World War I, he arrived in New York in 1921 full of excitement to have a shot at earning a living doing what he loved.

This book grew out of oral and written history—not only of my grandfather, but also written and oral histories of my grandmother and mother. I would like to thank writer Ross Goodner, who did an extensive interview with Bobby and gave his notes to my family. I researched newspapers of the times to confirm the stories. Some seemed improbable, such as the trip to an exhibition match in 1924. It was Bobby's first trip by air, and the biplane crashed on the landing, but he and Cyril Walker crawled out of the wreckage to play the exhibition.

I wrote this book to preserve what life was like, not just for the pro, but also for the pro's family in those times. Bobby had a deep respect and love for his fellow players as well as the game of golf. Much of this history seems unlikely in light of today's multimillion-dollar prizes, private jets, endorsements, and tournaments throughout the world, but the roots of this bonanza should not be forgotten. I hope this history might bring a shake of the head and a chuckle to a golfer today.

The Two Bobbys:
Jones and Cruickshank

The first meeting of Bobby Jones and Bobby Cruickshank was inauspicious. It happened in 1921 at the US Open at the Columbia Golf Club outside of Washington, DC. Cruickshank played a practice round with Alex Smith, former Open winner, and Bobby Jones. On the tenth hole, Jones hit an approach that just trickled over the back.

Cruickshank and Smith ducked as they heard a whirring over their heads. Jones had sent his club airborne in anger. Smith whispered to Cruickshank, "Don't say anything." He announced to Jones that he was amazed at the flock of gulls flying over their heads being so far from the sea. Jones looked to his feet, obviously embarrassed, but chipped close and got his par.

After the hole, in his Southern drawl, he apologized. "Y'all know I'm very sorry I threw that club."

Smith said, "That's okay, my boy. I've thrown caddies and clubs before."

He told Cruickshank that Jones was a great boy who would be a force in the game one day.

"Little did I know how right he was and how our paths would cross," Cruickshank said later.

It was at the 1921 US Open that he became a great admirer of Jones and his golfing ability. When they met again in the 1923 Open at Inwood Golf Club in New York, golf in America got a boost that would forever change the importance of the sport.

In the 1920s, golf in America was relatively new to the country and not fully embraced by the American people. The first impetus for golf came at the 1913 US Open when a young man who had been a caddy, Francis Ouimet, defeated Harry Vardon and Ted

Ray in a playoff. Vardon and Ray were from Britain and considered the best in the world.

People began to take notice of golf, and many started to play, even though some American businessmen thought it was a sinful waste of time.

By 1923, Bobby Jones had become a popular figure with his good looks, fine sportsmanship, and wonderful golf. However, he had not broken through. Golf fans were frustrated that he always seemed on the verge of greatness.

At Inwood Golf Club on Long Island, New York, the site of the 1923 US Open, the crowds were huge, and excitement stirred fans to a fever pitch. Paired together the first two days, Cruickshank and Jones found themselves tied. Rudy Knepper, a top amateur, saw the two Bobbys at the hotel that evening.

"Wouldn't it be nice if you fellows tied for the championship?" he said. Knepper's words were prophetic.

"That is just what we did," Cruickshank said.

On the final day when two rounds were played, a system for low scores to go out last did not exist, and Jones finished relatively early. In his final round he played the eighteenth hole badly, a treacherous long par four over water, but still was in a position to win. At least no one could beat him. Or so everyone thought. But Jones knew in golf, things could quickly change. He was correct.

Word came back to the clubhouse that Cruickshank had caught fire with nine holes to go and had a chance to catch Jones. Scotty Chisholm, a fellow Scot, excited that Cruickshank might win, asked for permission to play the bagpipes on the roof of the club house so he could pipe him home, but he wasn't allowed. Five thousand fans raced back onto the course to find Cruickshank.

Cruickshank's wife, Nellie, who always followed every hole, was having an enjoyable day with no problem seeing every shot, even at four foot eleven. All of a sudden, a tsunami of people scrambled over her, pushing, jostling as they ran over one another to get a vantage point. Crowd control didn't exist.

"I had to run like mad to see if the putts would go down," she said.

When Cruickshank double-bogeyed the sixteenth hole after a bad lie resulted in a poor chip, officials asked Jones if he wanted to go over to the prize table. He refused, saying he had not yet won. After a par on the seventeenth, Cruickshank needed to birdie the very difficult eighteenth to tie, a seemingly impossible task. He hit a beautiful drive. Cruickshank was paired with his friend Walter Hagen, who walked side by side with him to help tamp down the emotions of the eager golfer.

When Cruickshank got to his drive, he pulled out a long iron. The ball flew over the water in front of the green and landed six feet from the cup—six feet from a tie and a playoff. Reports said he struck the ball firmly into the center of the hole.

Nellie crawled between people's legs and got through just in time to see the putt drop for a playoff and a chance to win.

"That was the greatest thrill I ever had," she said. "That hole, the next day, was my greatest heartbreak."

Jones and Cruickshank tied at 296, the only two to break 300 on the difficult layout.

Bobby Jones spent the evening with his friend Francis Ouimet. Bobby Cruickshank spent the evening with Nellie and Walter Hagen trying to keep him at ease.

The next morning both men arrived on the first tee, nervous but eager, for the Open is a life-changing event. By a large margin, the ten thousand spectators rooted for Bobby Jones, as Cruickshank was largely unknown at the time. The Associated Press reported that the gallery was an "unruly mob that swarmed over both golfers and violated every rule of golf etiquette."

The match went back and forth through seventeen holes with only three holes halved. They stood on the eighteenth tee all tied up.

Cruickshank hit a poor drive. Nellie said she thought this resulted from breaking his wooden-shafted driver on his tee shot. Jones played the hole exactly as Cruickshank did the day before.

As a result of the poor drive, Cruickshank had to play short of the water. Many years later, as he remembered the playoff he said, "I can still hear the crack of that iron he hit." Rebel yells celebrating the young Georgian's win resonated in the air. Fans carried Jones off on their shoulders.

People lauded Cruickshank because of his brave tie the day before. They saw him as courageous, a great golfer, and a sportsman.

His sportsmanship was evident when an incident happened on the tenth hole of the playoff—an incident having nothing to do with Bobby Jones. An official stepped out on the green and challenged Cruickshank on how he brushed aside worm casts on the green. Cruickshank knew he was correct, as did the other officials and Jones who stood up for Cruickshank. Jones said Cruickshank was an honorable person, and the match should go on. However, Cruickshank, an emotional golfer, stewed inside for the next few holes.

To Cruickshank this was just fate. He also knew that handling adversity was something a champion needed to do.

Some of Cruickshank's fellow pros were upset, and a news article appeared the following day about the incident. Cruickshank refused to comment other than to say Jones was the better golfer that day, one of the best in the world, and deserved to win. Anyone who knew Cruickshank knew he meant it.

In his speech at the prize ceremony he said, "Oh but it was bonnie. My, what a golfer that boy is. He is the greatest champion of them all. He is Harry Vardon at his best and better than that. To be defeated by him is glory enough."

A moved Jones hugged his former foe. Jones said that this playoff was the greatest thrill in his career, and the two Bobbys remained good friends for the rest of their lives, forever bonded in golf history by that July day at Inwood in 1923.

Nellie had gone from elation after the birdie one day to disappointment the next.

She said, "I soon realized there would be many such disappointments, and if I was going to follow the events, I must school myself to accept the defeats as gracefully as the wins. I'd keep Bobby's morale up by reminding him there was always a next time."

In later years, Cruickshank said that Jones had a perfect swing with grace and rhythm. He also said Jones was wonderful to play with, as he "wrapped himself in the game, and you couldn't help but admire him. He brought out the good in others just by watching. He was perfection. We had a wonderful play-off, and I think I sent him on his winning ways."

Jones called Bobby's finish in the fourth round at Inwood "one of the greatest holes ever played in golf."

Cruickshank gained many admirers and was on his way to a successful career in golf. It was a life far away from his beginnings playing golf on makeshift holes in a field in the hardscrabble world of the Scottish Highlands, where a kick in the head by a grumpy horse changed his destiny.

Young Bobby

Grantown-on-Spey, a village on the River Spey in the north of Scotland, lies amidst the heathered hills, an ideal world to young Bobby Cruickshank. He loved the river, wide and black, where whitecaps bubbled as the rushing water met the rocks. The Spey, where he fished for salmon, was a short walk through the pine forest from town. The braw hills spelled freedom, the mist-shrouded Cairngorm Mountains wonder. The Highlands were where he wanted to be, where he would likely have spent his life, following his father into his carpentry work, maybe becoming club champion at the Grantown Golf Course like his dad. But fate intervened.

Bobby and his three young friends looked longingly at "the big course," the one they were too young to play. From a nearby field, they could watch the golfers. To make the best of things, they created three golf holes in the field by digging holes for cups.

Bobby said, "We played about 150 holes a day going round and round the three holes."

They shared the field with a grumpy old stallion they had to avoid. Bobby remembered the stallion "had the longest tail I'd ever seen."

Grantown-on-Spey, a popular summer retreat for well-to-do visitors from Edinburgh, bustled in those months. Both visitors and locals could take a shortcut through the field where the boys built their golf holes. Ten-year-old Bobby decided he would show off for the walkers. He grabbed the horse's tail and began to swing it back and forth. The horse quickly put an end to this with a swift kick, knocking Bobby out.

One of the visitors walking through the field was Mrs. Isabella Usher, a summer visitor from Edinburgh. She ran over to help

Bobby and got him to Dr. Barclay, the town doctor, staying there until she was sure he was all right. Then, she took him back to his parents.

It happened that Mrs. Usher was a wealthy widow of a brewing family in Edinburgh. She lived by herself in a large home in Murrayfield, having lost her husband a year or two before and her only child at age two. As she visited the Cruickshank home to check on Bobby, she also got to know his brother, John, who was a year and a half younger. She could see that the family did not have a lot of resources, and she recognized much potential in the boys. She offered to take them back to Edinburgh to live with her during the school year. In the summer they would return to Grantown to be with family.

Bobby's parents could not refuse such an offer and a chance for the boys. Bobby said Mrs. Usher was the most wonderful person, who became his second mother. She took them home to her house in Edinburgh and enrolled them in Daniel Stewart College, a private school in Edinburgh. In Grantown, school had been a punishment for Bobby, keeping him penned up away from his beloved hills and the river filled with salmon. Though he didn't like school, he did like John Stewart, the headmaster. Stewart, a good golfer, along with Bobby's father, taught him a lot about the game.

Although Bobby disliked attending school in Grantown, somehow Daniel Stewart College fit him well, and his years there were happy—most likely because of all the sports he got to play. He became an excellent sprinter, a good boxer, and a respected rugby and soccer player. In 1912, he did the hundred-yard dash in 10.4 seconds, and this record was not broken until 1960 by Sandy Hinshelwood, future rugby international. Bobby felt proud that he did 5'9" in the high jump, and at five foot four could walk back under the pole. In 1912, in the Interscholastic Games he won the hundred-yard dash, the long jump, and throwing the cricket ball (one hundred four yards, two feet, eight inches). He shared honors in the high jump.

But most of all he loved the golf matches he played. It was during his time at Daniel Stewart College that he met Tommy Armour, who attended another school. They met through competitions, and Tommy became his lifelong dearest friend—their friendship is known to have been close. "He helped me more than anyone in the world." As school chums, they played golf every chance they got. At Braid Hills, a course nestled high above Edinburgh, they trotted between shots and, according to Bobby, played seventy to eighty holes in a day. They also attended matches to see Harry Vardon, James Braid, J. H. Taylor, and George Duncan, where they learned by watching. Tommy's older brother, Sandy, helped teach them both.

During summers back in Grantown in his beloved Highlands, he filled his time with fishing and golf. Bobby's younger brother loved the Highlands, too, and looked up to his older brother, but he was not as driven by any particular sport. Bobby has said that John would have been a better golfer than he was if he wanted to be. But to the Cruickshank boys, if they died and went to heaven they knew it would be the Highlands in an eternal summer with their rugged hills and tumbling waters filled with salmon.

One summer when he was seventeen, Bobby decided to enter the open handicap tournament at the club. Being an open tournament, golfers from all over could play, making it an important event in the area. In one match he played a Reverend E. Shaw, who at six foot six was the biggest man Bobby had ever seen. At five foot four, Bobby and the Reverend must have been a comical sight on the course. With the reverend's five handicap, Bobby had to give him five shots. They ended the eighteen holes all even and had to go an extra hole. The reverend did not get a shot from him on that hole, and Bobby holed his putt. The reverend had a nine-inch putt to keep the match alive.

Bobby said, "I'll never forget that big man standing over that little putt. His hands were shaking like aspen leaves, and he missed that putt. Why I didn't concede it I'll never know."

In the finals, Bobby met John Stewart, his former headmaster at the local school. Bobby beat him, but he said, "He was so proud I beat him, you'd have thought he won. He went all over town boasting about how I beat him."

After Daniel Stewart College, Bobby and his friend Tommy went to the University of Edinburgh. Soon Bobby's brother, John, joined them. Bobby sat for law, but he did not like studying and being cooped up in classrooms. His Highland spirit clamored to get out. His chance came in 1914 when Britain went to war.

The War Years: 1914–1918

In 1914, young men in Britain were caught up in the patriotic fervor to fight for their country. Their youthful bravery and enthusiasm masked the realities of war. Bobby saw the war as an acceptable way out of the university, which he knew one day would consign him to a law office. He decided he would join the fight and deal with those responsibilities later.

What Bobby did, so did his admiring younger brother. Mrs. Usher worried about their safety and wanted to use her influence to get them commissions. Bobby inquired about things and heard that the lieutenants were often the first to be killed, so he and John went in as enlisted men. They joined the Seaforth Highlanders, the army of his homeland. He and John went to train in the Highlands near Elgin and the North Sea Flats. His best friend, Tommy, joined a tank regiment. Golf disappeared from their lives until the war ended in 1918. Tournaments were suspended for the duration of the war.

Bobby learned about shooting, hand-to-hand combat with bayonets, and trench warfare. None of this prepared him for the realities of war at the front. After completing his training, perhaps because of his athletic ability, Bobby's first assignment was to train new recruits, which he did through much of 1914 and 1915.

In 1916, replacements were needed so Bobby, his brother, and the Seaforth Highlanders became part of the Fifty-First Regiment, which also included the Black Watch, the Southern Highlanders, the Gordon Highlanders, and the Cameron Highlanders. The Germans called them the Ladies from Hell, because they wore kilts. Bobby described that this was when he learned what war really was. The noise, the smell, and the carnage stayed with him for the rest of his life. He and his brother were sent to the trenches, which Bobby could never speak about other than to shake his head. He said the half-moon trenches, which were begun in 1917, changed the war. Soldiers stayed for three to four weeks until replacements came. Then they rotated back to become the replacements. He fought through Somme, Ypres, and Passchendaele, where three hundred thousand lost their lives. In one battle, eleven hundred of them went out and fewer than three hundred returned. He said he knew what hell must be like, and he never forgot the taste of cordite in the air.

"I could feel it in my mouth," he said. For the rest of his life he would sometimes wake up screaming, always on a battlefield like Ypres, Somme, or Passchendaele. Bobby said they were all "scared as hell."

Then a tragedy struck that impacted his life forever. At Ypres, his brother John and his platoon fought about fifty yards away from Bobby and his group. The fighting raged fierce and nonstop for thirty minutes.

Bobby said, "Shells were bursting everywhere and you could really smell the damned cordite, you could feel it in your mouth. When the barrage lifted, there were 78 of our company killed out of 110, and my brother was one of them. There had been thousands of shells and everything was covered up."

When they were able to get out of the trenches, he searched frantically for John, but he found no sign of his beloved younger brother, "yet he had been as close to me as from here to that door." Out of John's platoon only one soldier survived, and that soldier had nineteen shrapnel wounds. Bobby always felt it should have been him and not his little brother.

Bobby also received wounds in the battle. Shrapnel shred his leg, and because of the fighting, they couldn't get him out until the next day. His leg became infected, and he was sent to the hospital at Blighty, then to Ireland for convalescence.

He loved Ireland and its people. When given a night out, he and a friend met an old gentleman at the pub who invited them back to his home for "real Irish stew." After being AWOL for two days, they got into trouble. Bobby's wound was so bad that it should have meant being released from the army, but things were not going well and Britain needed more troops.

Bobby got sent back to the front. Who knows how to measure these young men whose lives, if not lost, were suspended for the war years? Bobby and Tommy, two of Scotland's best golfers, had no opportunity to play the game they loved. Golf was just a remembrance in the dank mist of the battlefield, and one can only speculate what might have been. Bobby was twenty in 1914 when he entered the war and would not get back to golf until 1919.

But it was 1917 and the war continued. Bobby was to have an improbable adventure of capture and eventual escape.

Soon after returning to the front, Bobby's platoon came under siege. The Germans surrounded them, and Bobby's men were out of ammunition, food, and water for almost three days with no communication. Bobby, as sergeant, went out to see what he could find or where they could go. In the pitch-black night, Bobby could make out a figure.

He called, "What is your battalion?"

The soldier yelled, "Shotlander."

Bobby knew he was in trouble. He said the German soldier was scared as he was at first, but soon other German soldiers arrived. Bobby was now a prisoner of war.

After processing and interrogation, Bobby was sent to Arras in the south of France to an old camp the soldiers called Fort MacDonald, which held about seven thousand prisoners. Bobby found himself in a room twenty by forty feet with forty to fifty men in the room. Fate intervened again, for in the room was Sandy Armour, suffering from a bad case of dysentery.

"We were fed once a day like a dog," Bobby recalled. Each prisoner got a quarter of a loaf of black bread and a bowl of soup. He shared his food with Sandy. Sometimes Bobby found a dead horse when out on work detail, which he cut up for meat. He helped Sandy get up and down stairs to the latrine. With Bobby's help, Sandy recovered. Sandy and Tommy both believed Bobby saved Sandy's life.

Since Bobby knew a little German, he was tapped to be an interpreter. Despite the war, the German soldiers in the prison treated them with humanity. The Red Cross came weekly with mail and took requests. Sandy had been an orchestra leader in Britain and played the violin very well. He asked for a violin, never expecting to get one. To his surprise one arrived. The German soldiers enjoyed his playing, and he performed a weekly concert. He tapped Bobby to be his assistant.

As a result of this, they did not get the worst jobs, except once. They were sent out on the barrel detail. About forty prisoners trooped to an old battlefield to dig up and find the remains of soldiers. They had to put the remains in coffins. The only salvation was the schnapps they got, which they needed to keep from passing out. That day the prisoners and the guards drank every drop of schnapps becoming, as Bobby said, "cock-eyed drunk." It was about ten to twelve kilometers back to the camp, and the prisoners and guards arrived arm in arm, singing. Some of the prisoners carried the rifles.

The soldiers at the camp laughed until a spit-and-polish officer gave them a right good dressing down. The officer had been educated at Oxford. He said the prisoners were a disgrace to the British army. The guards got sent to the Russian front. Sandy and Bobby lost their cushy jobs and found themselves permanently on work detail.

In 1918, the war took a turn for the worse for Germany. The Americans joined the fight and the Germans were pushed back toward Brussels. About 2,500 weak prisoners, including Bobby and Sandy, marched back along with the German army. They had to march twenty to twenty-five kilometers a day, a march of invalids. Guards prodded the weak and staggering soldiers along. When they arrived in Brussels, the entire town came out to cheer the prisoners on. They threw food—bread, cheese, and whatever they could—to the men. The guards could do nothing with only one guard for every twenty-five to thirty prisoners. The Belgians' generosity gave Bobby hope and helped them all continue. "The

Belgian people could not do enough for us and they risked their lives every minute with us."

At their new camp, about 1,200 prisoners went out each day to pick beets. They left the camp at 5:00 a.m. and arrived at the fields at 8:00 a.m. They worked all day going up one row and down the next until dusk when they marched three hours back. Bobby had noticed a change in the guards' attitudes. They were friendlier and helped the prisoners forage for food, even sharing what they found, which told Bobby the war wasn't going well for them. Bobby made contact with the Belgian woman who owned the farm on which they picked beets. She spoke perfect English, having lived in Yorkshire for years. He let her know he wanted to escape. It just so happened she was in the Belgian underground. One day she pointed to a tiny tool shed in the field. She told Bobby when he got a chance to get into the shed and wait for her. Bobby, Ferguson, a fellow Scot, and two Englishmen managed to get to the shed unnoticed.

The woman and her daughter led them at night to a little town about three miles away. She gave them boiled milk and bread, which Bobby said was like a king's feast. She provided a map and a letter of introduction to her uncle in another village. They took off when it got dark, traveling until the gray streaks of dawn appeared. To their horror, they found they were back where they started, having traveled in a circle.

"It almost broke our hearts," Bobby said.

In later years if he got lost driving and Nellie told him to ask for directions, he always replied, "I bloody well found my way through Belgium."

After this disappointment, they went back to the Belgian woman, who, at great risk to herself, led them about eight kilometers to the correct road. Bobby said he heard this woman had helped 168 soldiers escape. He and Ferguson told the authorities about her when he finally got back home, and he heard she got a medal from the government.

The thought of freedom kept him going. Eventually, he,

Ferguson, and the two Englishmen found the refuge covered with brush and sticks in the field. They entered it and went down about fifteen feet to a room with food and drink.

Bobby said they marched a total of three nights and, according to Bobby, were about fifty kilometers from Brussels. The last night, when they got to a small town, they realized they had marched too long. Light filtered in and they ran into a German patrol. The two English prisoners, about fifty yards ahead, yelled "Jerrys" and ran. They had been discovered by the German patrol. Bobby and Ferguson dove into a canal and hid in the reeds. Bobby said he thought the two Englishmen were either shot or captured, but the Germans did not know there were two others.

He and Ferguson stayed among the reeds in the canal all day, an uncomfortable place for two men who couldn't swim. At night they arrived at a small town with a bridge, which was guarded by two German soldiers. They slipped back into the canal until a Belgian man came along pushing a wheelbarrow with a large sack in it. Bobby took a chance and used his French to whisper, "Monsieur." The man stopped. Bobby told him they were escaped prisoners. It turned out that the man's name was Jacques, and he was about twenty years old. He was in the process of stealing corn from the Germans. He told Bobby and Ferguson to follow him home and hid them in a hayloft.

Bobby said they slept on about "thirty tons of hay with a blanket above and below us. We slept all day. At night Jacque brought us down to the house and we had supper. That was the best meal and the best sleep I ever had. He and his mother gave us clothes, a scarf, and a change of underclothes, the first in seven months. We also each got a pair of wooden clogs. We were now Belgians."

Jacques and his mother knew when the German patrol came through each day. When it was safe, Bobby and Ferguson could come down and join them in their home. Bobby said that Jacques's mother was a dear old soul and had no use for the Germans. They stayed about a week going to homes of friends and family in the evenings where Ferguson impressed them with his Scottish songs. One night Jacques asked them if they'd like to go to town for a couple of steins of beer. Of course they did. Jacques warned them not to speak, and they entered a tiny bar and ordered the brews.

"We tasted our first beer since being captured, and needless to say, we tried to make up for lost time."

Six German soldiers came in and started drinking. Jacques, concerned about being discovered, whispered to drink up and get going. Unfortunately, Ferguson was feeling good and shouted, "Here's luck" to Jacques, who quickly doused the lights with the beer and they all ran—Bobby and Ferguson back into the canal.

Jacques was able to convince the soldiers that he had never seen Bobby and Ferguson before. The soldiers searched but could not find them even though the whole town knew of their presence. Bobby and Ferguson were able to make their way back to the farm, the loft, and safety. However, Jacques said that after the incident he was under watch, and their activities were more limited than ever.

They learned the Allies and the British Eighty-Eighth Regiment were about eight kilometers away. The Germans were ragtag and retreating. One day an unarmed German private arrived at the kitchen door. "He was bedraggled, poor little soul. He said, 'Wasser, wasser.' so I gave him a scoop. He didn't know I was a prisoner of war."

With the front so close, Bobby and Ferguson said goodbye to Jacques and his mother, who kissed them and cried. Bobby said, "She had been like a mother to us, and I felt a lump come up in my throat when we left them to make for the front lines." He and Ferguson kept in contact with the woman and her son after the war and sent the mother some money to help with her old age.

They got to a village filled with German soldiers. Bobby and Ferguson, dressed as civilians, were ordered inside a store.

Bobby said, "An old couple there heard our story and gave us food. At about ten in the morning all hell broke loose, and a machine gun fight broke out. We saw the Germans break and run as the Allies entered the town. All of a sudden everything stopped, and a great shout went up. Armistice had been signed and the war was over. Ferguson and I ran over to an officer and threw our arms around him cheering hysterically in English. I was upset when I saw his rank. He was General Freyberg of the Eighty-Eighth Brigade. He was the same General Freyberg who later came within half a mile of swimming the English Channel. This was not bad for someone wounded on ten different occasions, which I had seen by the chevrons he wore. He told a soldier to take us for some Scotch."

Bobby and Ferguson went by train to Dieppe with other freed prisoners and boarded a hospital ship. He remembers sailing into South Hampton with thousands of people tooting horns and shouting as ten thousand prisoners debarked, home at last. The war was good and truly over. Now Bobby had to decide what to do with the rest of his life.

After the War

After the war ended, thousands of young men came home. Jobs were scarce. Bobby did not want to return to the university, as he thought he was too old. He took a civil service course and passed the exam, but at the interview he found the job would not be available for fifteen months.

Mrs. Usher had passed away and left Bobby an inheritance of about £10,000, which gave him breathing room. Before the war Bobby met his wife-to-be, Nellie Cumming, through her father and brothers who were excellent golfers. He married Nellie when he returned from the war, and soon she would be having a baby. Nellie's family belonged to Turnhouse Golf Club in Edinburgh, which Bobby joined when he took up golf again. He did not consider golf as a career, for pros in Britain didn't rank very highly. Bobby, if he were a pro, would not be admitted into the clubhouse of the course where he enjoyed a membership. However, he did start to play in amateur tournaments. He won the Edinburgh Coronation Cup in 1919, an important tournament, and was low amateur in the French Open. He set a course record of sixty at the newly opened Queens's course at Gleneagles, where he had a female caddy with the unfortunate nickname of Smelly Nelly. His wife, Nellie, who shared her name, remembers that when they left the clubhouse to go home, Smelly Nelly was taking on all challengers who said Bobby could not have shot a sixty. He also set course records with a sixty-three at Turnhouse and a sixty-eight at Muirfield.

One day at Turnhouse, while playing with his father-in-law, he met the man who interviewed him for the civil service job. He said that when Bobby reported he had a plus-four handicap, he ruined his chances of getting a position sooner, as this meant he spent too much time on the golf course.

Bobby's best friend, Tommy Armour, had also been wounded in the war, losing sight in one eye. After the war, Tommy went to America as a representative for a rubber company in 1919. He returned and told Bobby opportunities abounded in the United States.

Bobby also played golf with Willie Parks Jr., a former British Open champion, who encouraged him to go and try golf in the States. Parks had been over before the war, building golf courses. After one game, he gave Bobby his Tom Stewart putter, the one he used to win the Open, and that was the putter Bobby used in his match with Bobby Jones in 1923. Many years later in 1949, Bobby became head pro at Chartiers Country Club in Pittsburgh, Pennsylvania, a course designed by Willie Parks Jr.

One day, soon after that Turnhouse golf game with Parks, Bobby decided he was ready to take a chance and see if he could make a life in America.

Nellie recalled, "Bobby came bursting through the door and asked me if I would like to go to America to live. Being young and in love, I said yes."

So Bobby, Nellie, and their new baby Elsie, booked passage on the *Algeria* in March.

The *Algeria*, a small ship, had been Kaiser Wilhelm's personal yacht. Another pro, Willie Anderson, happened to be aboard, and he gave Bobby some contacts in America. Great golfer-to-be thirteen-year-old Jimmy Thompson also traveled to the States with his family. They planned to join his father, who was pro at the Country Club of Virginia. In 1932, Bobby would end up there as head pro. The three golfers occupied their time on the ship hitting balls into the ocean on the very rough crossing, where most passengers were ill and didn't venture on deck. In fact, Nellie was so sick Bobby cared for Elsie on the journey. Jimmy Thompson became one of the game's longest hitters, won many tournaments, and married Viola Dana, a beautiful film star.

The *New York Times* reported on April 10, 1921, that Bobby Cruickshank, one of Britain's top amateurs, arrived in America to make it his home. Bobby said that he and his family easily breezed through Ellis Island thanks to his inheritance, which proved he could support his family.

Bobby and Nellie planned to give it six months before deciding whether to stay permanently and make golf his career. Becoming a pro was not an easy decision. Bobby and Tommy had been good amateur players in Britain. Having gone to college, they had followed an unusual path to becoming a pro. Most golf pros came through the caddy ranks. American newspapers referred to Bobby and Tommy, when he later turned pro, as Joe College men. Reporters marveled that they saw golf as honorable a business as law or medicine. But Father John B. Kelly in *American Golfer Magazine* in 1921 said that golf was a good influence and kept men away from becoming "lounge lizards and corpulent toddy bibbers."

Some businessmen looked on earning money playing golf with suspicion. One editorial in the Davenport, Iowa, newspaper in 1923 claimed that winning a golf tournament got one pro a wealthy wife, which never would have happened if he hadn't won the event. The United States Golf Association (USGA) also had concerns about clubs offering too much money for winning a tournament. They worried this would create a class of golfers who would do nothing but play in golf tournaments.

However, unlike pros in Britain, pros in America enjoyed more acceptance.

Bobby decided to play in a few golf tournaments before making a commitment to stay. Nellie and Bobby booked a room at the Commodore Hotel in New York. Bobby learned that the A. G. Spalding Company in the city was a meeting place for many of the pros, and he went most days to spend time meeting people. One of these people was Dave Hunter, pro at Essex Golf Club in West Orange, New Jersey. He needed an assistant, and he took a liking to Bobby. He invited Bobby to his course to play with him and the club president, a Mr. Hoffman, who approved of Bobby after the game. Dave Hunter offered him the job. Bobby said to

Hunter, "I know how to play a little, but I don't know a damn thing about teaching or club repair or anything like that."

Hunter said all that could be learned, and Bobby accepted the job as his assistant, which sealed Bobby's decision to stay.

Nellie packed up and they went to West Orange to be nearer work. They wanted to rent a room at a Mrs. Smith's, but she did not want to rent to a family with a baby. Nellie looked so tiny and sad that Mrs. Smith invited them in for some tea. After the tea, Mrs. Smith changed her mind and rented them a room. The Smiths became like a second family to Bobby and Nellie, taking care of Elsie when Bobby and Nellie traveled to the western tournaments in the winter.

So the Cruickshank family settled in.

"I'll never forget the first lesson I gave," Bobby said later. "It was to Mr. Rand of the Remington Rands. It was for a half an hour, but an hour and a half later I said, 'Mr. Rand, I think I don't know what the hell I'm doing.' He was so nice and said that since I was honest, he would take a half-hour lesson every morning except Sunday, and we could both learn together. Mr. Hoffman also hired me to give him some lessons to give me more experience in teaching before they turned me loose on the other members."

Although a pro needed a club job to survive since prize money was small and tournaments were few and far between, clubs liked their pros to play in tournaments to represent them. A pro was introduced on the first tee as "Bobby Cruickshank representing the Essex Golf Club." Bobby was able, in fact encouraged, to play in tournaments. His first tournament was at Shawnee, Delaware. Bobby didn't do well but got some experience.

The next one was the 1921 US Open at Columbia Golf Club outside of Washington, DC, where along with Bobby Jones, he met Freddy McLeod, Jock Hutchinson, and Jim Barnes, three older Scottish pros. Bobby spoke of their kindness to him, showing him the ropes of being a pro.

Jim Barnes won the Open at Columbia, but Bobby made a decent showing.

Next, he went to Syracuse to play in the New York State Open. On the last day, paired with Jack Forrester, Bobby thought he had to make a four-foot putt to win, which would help seal his reputation as a top golfer in the States.

He said, "I couldn't see the ground, the ball, the hole, or anything. My knees shook, my mouth felt dry, but I holed the putt. I didn't have the correct information and found I won by eight shots. Walter Hagen was second, and Jim Barnes was fourth or fifth." The New York Open was the first tournament he won in America, and beating Hagen and Barnes, who had just won the US Open, brought him the recognition he hoped for.

Bobby said, "It was there I got to know Walter Hagen, who became a dear friend. Not only was he a great player but one of the finest men I ever met on the golf course. He was a great thinker and took everything so calmly. He never got excited and didn't take chances. He had the greatest golf mind of anyone I knew. Hagen did many charitable things he never got credit for."

At the 1921 PGA Championship at Inwood, the club where Bobby later met Jones in 1923, pros stayed at the hotel at Grand Central Station and took the train out to the course. They enjoyed chatting on the way. When someone asked Jock Hutchinson, a British Open champion, whom he was playing he said, "Some little fellow named Sarazen." The little fellow beat him eight and seven. Hutchinson had to endure lots of kidding on the way back.

Bobby also lost eight and seven to Jim Barnes in the thirty-six-hole match. Bobby said, "He was just too good for me." Hagen went on to win the tournament.

After the PGA, Bobby went to St. Joseph, Missouri, for a tournament. He shot a sixty-nine the last day and tied Jim Barnes and Jock Hutchinson. They decided on a nine-hole playoff since the two stars had to catch a train for an exhibition.

Bobby shot thirty-four to thirty-seven by Hutchinson and thirty-nine by Jim Barnes. Bobby won $1,000 and $100 for the lowest round of the tournament (sixty-nine). He received good publicity, beating the current US champion and a British Open champion. By winning two tournaments he established himself as a top player and was offered the job of head professional at Shackamaxon in Westfield, New Jersey.

In 1922, he won three other tournaments: the Capital City Open in Washington, DC, a tournament in New Jersey, and a Spalding tournament at Wakagyl where Cyril Walker and Johnny Farrell tied for second. Bobby won by five shots and tied the course record with a seventy-one.

Bobby got to the semifinals of the PGA at Oakmont in 1922, losing to Gene Sarazen. Although he was one under par the first eighteen, he found himself four down. He was one or two under for the thirty-six-hole match, but lost four and two.

He liked Sarazen, who was not much bigger than him. "He was one of the finest players I ever saw. I respect him very much, indeed, and he is a thorough gentleman. He had confidence in his ability and proved he deserved it."

Bobby also played some golf with Leo Diegel, who was the personal pro for Edward B. McLean, owner of the *Washington Post*. McLean built a course of eighteen holes with seventeen greens within his walled-in estate in Washington, DC, on Wisconsin Avenue.

President Warren Harding was an avid golfer and played many games there. Bobby was invited to play and said that even though prohibition was the law of the land, liquor "flowed like water in a fountain."

Bobby's career got off to a good start, and he never looked back. Because of his play, he could get exhibitions, which helped the bottom line. Exhibitions loomed large in a pro's life and also in the development of golf's popularity. Exhibitions were the only way many golf fans could see the players they read about in the papers. The match results generated headlines in papers across the country. Usually, tickets cost a dollar, and players often played for the gate. In 1922, Bobby played exhibitions with Sarazen in Detroit against two of Detroit's best players. They also played against Hagen and his partner and won. Bobby and

Sarazen played exhibitions in Syracuse, Bar Harbor, and in the Metropolitan area. In 1922, Bobby also went to Chicago to team with Bobby Jones against Hagen and Kirkwood.

Hagen, the only pro who took the chance to support himself with golf, succeeded because of his great showmanship. For example, Hagen arranged a match against Sarazen, which he billed as the unofficial championship of the world, generating great interest and publicity. If the exhibition involved players from Britain, the event was billed as defending the country's honor.

The following year, 1923, would seal Bobby's place in golf history, and because of a brilliant young Bobby Jones, golf would never be the same. It seems almost incomprehensible today that a pro golfer's main goal was to get a good club job. But in the 1920s an official tour didn't exist, and what tournaments there were offered little prize money. There were no lucrative deals representing golf equipment or other products. But Bobby was doing what he loved, and he was on his way.

On His Way: 1924

After the 1923 Open playoff, golf took off as a major sport. Golf courses were being built all over the country, and a pro could get a good job for his golf ability. With the positive attention Bobby got from his courageous play in the 1923 Open, he received an offer to become pro at a new club, Twin Oaks, in Oklahoma City. It was 1924, and he would make $10,000 a year. Bobby moved there with his family, but the course was not ready. He was free to play in tournaments and exhibitions representing the club.

The first week of June in 1924, Oakland Hills in Detroit hosted the US Open. Cyril Walker, a fellow pro, approached Bobby and asked if he would like to go fifty-fifty with him on winnings. This practice was not unusual in those days, because pros paid their own way, and there were no sponsors unless their home club chipped in. However, Bobby said no to Walker, saying it was the US Open. Bobby said, "We would lean on each other and maybe not do our best. If we are alone, we can do better, I think."

Walker went on to win the tournament, receiving $500. Bobby Jones was second, Bill Mehlhorn third, and Bobby tied for fourth with Walter Hagen and Macdonald Smith, each receiving $115.

Walker, born in England, was a small man weighing no more than 130 pounds. He had never before won an important title. He earned the reputation of being the slowest player in the game.

Westbrook Pegler wrote in a column that on the eighteenth hole Walker came "charging down the fairway at the sensational pace of a senile snail." Walker played the last nine in even par to beat Bobby Jones on the hard course in high winds, which made it especially difficult for a small man.

As Open champion, Walker could arrange exhibitions. He

asked Bobby if he'd like to join him on the tour he was setting up, and Bobby agreed, happy to do this as it was an opportunity to earn good money.

Bobby and Walker played exhibitions in Sioux City, Iowa; North Platte, Nebraska; and Fort Dodge, Colorado. At one stop in Peoria, Illinois, officials cancelled a baseball game between Peoria and Terre Haute, Indiana, so the townspeople could go out and see the golfers. Bobby and Walker played against top amateur Chick Evans and P. F. Carter, a former Irish champion. Evans said that no one regretted the cancellation of the game, and even the ballplayers came out to watch.

It was on July 27, 1924, at one of these exhibitions in Janesville, Wisconsin, that Bobby and Walker almost lost their lives.

One of the stops was in Minneapolis, Minnesota. Bobby broke the course record, and the members invited them to stay for the dance that evening to celebrate. How could they refuse? They believed there were three trains to Janesville, and they could catch the last one later in the evening.

Bobby enjoyed a bit of Scotch, especially in the relaxed exhibition circuit when being absolutely sharp was not vital. However, Walker, according to Bobby, loved his Scotch any time. They both partied that night, dancing and telling stories. Then . . .

Bobby looked at the time. "Cyril," he said, "we have to go or we'll miss the train."

They arrived at the station with some revelers and found there wasn't a late train after all.

"Not to worry," said one of the partygoers. "I have a plane, and I'll fly you there in plenty of time."

Bobby and Walker were unsure about this, since neither had flown before.

"Don't worry," said another gentleman. "You couldn't be in better hands. He was an ace pilot in the war."

They telegraphed the club at Janesville to say they'd arrive by air at one o'clock.

They planned to leave at ten thirty the next morning for a

two-and-a-half-hour flight to get there in time for the two o'clock exhibition.

The next morning Walker grabbed a bottle of Scotch, and they loaded their clubs and suitcases in the car. When they arrived at the airfield, a biplane sat before them like a giant dragonfly.

"Where will we put our clubs and bags?" asked Bobby, suddenly quite sober.

"We'll strap the golf bags on the wings, and your luggage can go in the plane with you," said the ace.

"You both can fit in the seat. Might be a little crowded, but it's just two and a half hours." Bobby and Walker, both small men, agreed that it was not impossible.

Bobby decided this adventure might be fun after all as the golf bags were safely strapped on the wings. An unsmiling and quiet Walker climbed in.

The plane took off and ascended into the air.

"Look Cyril," said Bobby. "Look down at the water."

"Forget the bloody water. Where's my Scotch?"

Bobby looked over at Walker who was white as a new golf ball. His hands clutched the struts, and he only pried his hands off to take a spine stiffener of Scotch.

They put down at La Crosse to refuel and took off again. Unfortunately, a storm arose and put them forty miles off course.

Bobby heard, *Sput, sput, sput . . .*

"We're out of gas," yelled the pilot. "We have to put down."

Walker's eyes widened as his bloodless knuckles continued to grip the struts.

The pilot drifted down onto a farmyard. Pigs scattered as the plane bumped to a stop in their mud spa.

The farmer and his wife ran out.

Walker grabbed his bottle and took another swig of his beloved Scotch.

The pilot hopped down.

"We'll never get to the exhibition," grumbled Walker. "I've never missed an obligation in my life."

"We'll get some gas and soon be on our way," said the pilot.

The farmer told the pilot they could get gas at a neighbor's farm, so the pilot and farmer jumped in the farmer's truck and raced away.

"Bloody plane," said Walker. "We should have taken the train."

The farmer's wife made them coffee as they waited.

When the farmer and the pilot returned, along with the neighbor and his family, the pilot put gas in the plane. Some fencing had to be removed so the plane could take off. They waved goodbye as Walker took some more bracers of Scotch.

"We're almost there," called the pilot.

Meanwhile, at the course, despite threatening weather, hundreds of people arrived. They had each paid a dollar for a ticket to watch the two stars play two local pros, Jack Burgess of Lake Geneva and Marty Cromb, pro at Janesville. Two o'clock, the exhibition time, came and went with no golfers. Spectators searched the skies. Frank Sinclair, reporter for the *Janesville Daily Gazette*, described what was happening at the course.

"Every drone that had the slightest familiarity to the purr of an airplane, every speck in the sky, even a weathervane, was mistaken for the transport of air."

When four o'clock rolled around with no golf stars, the two local pros decided to tee it up. The officials offered a refund to the gallery and most left, as did the out-of-town reporters. As the two locals prepared to tee it up, someone sighted a plane for real and a cheer arose.

Officials tried to clear the fairway so the plane could land, but Bobby said the pilot felt there were still too many people in the way.

Then, *sput, sput, sput . . .*

"We're out of gas. I'll have to put it down in this field."

Bobby saw a train chugging along the track as they drifted down.

"We're going to hit the train!" Bobby yelled, for the first time feeling afraid.

They narrowly missed the train. The pilot planned to put down the plane on an oat field below.

Spectators rushed to their cars to get out to the landing site.

The pilot drifted down and jockeyed along, when he unexpectedly hit a ditch, flipping the plane nose down into the earth. Bobby heard a splintering sound, and he felt himself hanging upside down. Not knowing if Cyril and the pilot were hurt, he called out, "Are you all right?"

The pilot answered that he was all right, but there was no word from Cyril. Bobby struggled to crawl out of the upside-down plane, fearing the worst for Walker. When he emerged, he could not believe what he saw. Cyril was holding court, surrounded by the rescuers from the golf course, with no apparent thought for Bobby or the pilot.

"I'm Cyril Walker, the Open champion. Where are my clubs?"

The splintering sound was the propeller and a wing. All were shaken up, but no one was badly hurt other than some bruises. How the pilot dealt with his smashed plane and found his way back to Minneapolis is unknown. After all, the important matter was the upcoming golf match.

Officials bustled the golfers into cars and rushed to the course. Sinclair wrote, "Most men would have had nicked nerves, but the stars merely changed from street clothes to 'plus fours,' partook of a luncheon, and sallied forth to victory."

He went on to say that those who stayed saw wonderful golf. Bobby and Walker won three up. They finished just as darkness settled in with spotters sent forward to find the balls in the dusk. Walker tied the course record with sixty-eight, a record previously set by Chick Evans, and almost had a hole in one. Bobby later said that he couldn't see "the bloody ground," but still shot a seventy-two.

The officials were most thankful that Bobby and Walker only took the gate, which was less than a hundred dollars. Although Bobby and Walker lost money on this exhibition, they got word while they were there that exhibitions for the next two weeks were set and would net them a nice sum.

The next morning, the Janesville paper headlined "Walker Steps from Wrecked Plane and Equals Record."

At home, Nellie opened the morning paper to see in the national news that Bobby had been in a plane crash. Headlines reported that their plane crashed and turned over as they landed in Janesville. Panicked, she called hospitals in the area to find out if Bobby was all right.

He hadn't called to tell her because he didn't want her to worry. Meanwhile, he and Walker were on their way to the next exhibition—this time by train.

The following day they had an exhibition in Illinois with Chick Evans and Jock Hutchinson to help Chick Evans's caddy scholarship fund. Evans, who had remained an amateur going into business for his career, had been a caddy. He never forgot the young boys who toted the clubs for golfers and worked to help them all his life. When he went to a tournament, he always stopped by the caddy shack to talk with the boys.

Bobby and Walker lost, but Bobby wasn't surprised after the crash the day before. An auction after the exhibition raised more money for the fund. Chick Evans's driver went for a hundred dollars, Jock Hutchinson's mashie brought forty dollars, Bobby's mashie went for fifty dollars, and Walker's putter, the one he used to win the Open, brought fifty dollars.

While on the tour, they played in some tournaments if they were convenient. Bobby won the Mid Continent Open in Wichita, Kansas, shooting a 274 for seventy-two holes played over two days. Bobby set a course record of sixty-four in one round. Hagan was a distant second at 282, Joe Kirkwood third, and Leo Diegel fourth. Bobby also won the Colorado Open at Cherry Hills with Jock Hutchinson finishing second and Bill Mehlhorn third.

Unfortunately, the course in Oklahoma did not open as scheduled because of turf issues.

However, it was in Oklahoma City that Nellie had her first and only foray into competitive golf in America. Bobby planned to play in a tournament and decided she should stay home. Nellie was not pleased. She had a good golfing pedigree, and sometimes played in Scotland with her father and brothers in foursome matches at Turnhouse in Edinburgh. She understood the game as well as anyone. It so happened that the Oklahoma City Championship for ladies was being held the week Bobby was away. Nellie decided to show him and entered the competition.

She qualified for the B flight, as did the defending champion who had an unusually poor qualifying score for her. Nellie, at four foot eleven, was dwarfed by the rather large former champ, who was quite put out having to play in the B flight. Nellie met the former champion in the finals. Tiny Nellie found herself one up as they approached the ninth hole at the clubhouse. Out of the blue, with people looking on, the disgruntled former champ fainted in the bunker. After being revived, she continued on. Nellie, unperturbed by this incident, won the match.

When Bobby arrived home, Nellie didn't say a word about the trophy sitting on the table. She didn't have to. She had done better than Bobby, and she was quite pleased about it.

But what to do in the winter months loomed over the pros with great importance. The golfers had to find ways to earn money. Tournaments in Florida and out west provided the answer.

The Beginning
of the Golden Journey

The winter of 1924–1925 was a year before the Los Angeles Open with the unheard-of $10,000 purse, which started the "gold rush" to the West Coast. But in the winter and spring months of 1924–1925, Florida was the place to be, thanks to developer D. P. Davis, who hoped to make Florida the winter capital of golf. He thought that a golf league with teams of two golfers representing resorts in different parts of the state would function much like baseball, with teams building rivalries and local pride.

For $15,000, he brought over Archie Compston from England and Armand Massy from France. He hired Bobby and Johnny Farrell to form the team representing his development in Tampa. He provided the entire $5,000 purse for the Florida Open as well as helping promote other tournaments in the state.

Bobby and Johnny Farrell not only formed the Tampa team for the golf league, but they also gave exhibitions and taught Davis. On February 16, Bobby and Farrell beat Walter Hagen and Joe Kirkwood two and one in an eighteen-hole best ball. They did well in the matches, and at the end of the season played Leo Diegel and Gene Sarazen for the league championship. Bobby and Farrell won one up on the thirty-ninth hole. Westbrook Pegler noticed the golfers dressed in colorful clothes. Johnny Farrell became known as the Beau Brummel of the tour for his fashionable looks. Pegler also noted with some disdain that pros now were able to play exclusive clubs without paying greens fees.

Bobby and Johnny toured the state in Farrell's snazzy car. On one occasion they came upon an old Model T. "Pass him, Johnny. Show that old car what a real car can do," suggested Bobby. Johnny sped around the seemingly old crate. Unfortunately, the old crate was the souped-up car of the local sheriff. They were taken to jail and had to pay a hefty fine.

The golf league was a financial failure as fans lost interest. The pros did not like the way it affected their chance for organizing more lucrative exhibitions. To make matters worse, Florida had a severe cold spell in the winter, so cold that Gene Tunney couldn't practice boxing in the outdoor arena. Golfers huddled around fires.

Bobby and the other pros admired Davis, who loved golf and those who played it. His dream was a development off the Tampa coast called Davis Islands. He planned to keep supporting golf, but on October 12, 1926, he was lost at sea. He and his young son had traveled on the White Star Line *Majestic* to meet his wife in Paris. He enjoyed entertaining and stayed up until the early morning hours. The sea was rough one night, and in the early morning hours, Davis apparently fell overboard and was lost. The ship circled for an hour, but he was never seen again. Reports differ about what might have happened.

Despite the tragedy, golf in Florida continued to grow and remained an important part of the winter tour. Prize money increased, and in the winter of 1925–1926, the golden journey began in January with the Los Angeles Open. The pros then started the trek back east traveling to Texas, up to Hot Springs, down to Florida, and back up to the year's coveted finale, the North and South, in Pinehurst, North Carolina. That event took place in April, after which the pros returned to their clubs and the summer tournaments. The total purse for the winter tournaments in 1925–1926 was $22,500. Most tournaments had purses of at least a thousand dollars. However, some could be less, especially the tournaments that popped up unexpectedly. In those tournaments, the pros played for the gate, but with expenses high, the pros appreciated the chance to add to the coffers. Tommy Armour said that there was no purse too small for a golf pro.

The unheard-of purse of $10,000 proved so exciting that some pros talked about hiring a special railroad car to take them out.

This did not happen, but the pros planned to travel together. On December 7, 1925, pros in the Metropolitan area boarded the premier train of the time, the Twentieth Century Limited, to start their journey. They would begin their quest with the Monterrey Peninsula Open, Sacramento, and Long Beach, finally reaching Los Angeles for the crown jewel, the $10,000 open. The winter of 1926 marked the beginning of a new era in the sport.

THE CRUICKSHANK FAMILY

Bobby (Photo by George Pietzcker)

Nellie
(Photo by George Pietzcker)

Elsie

Bobby (far left) and his fellow "architects"
who made three golf holes in a local field.

1922 exhibition in Nashville with English golfer Abe Mitchell. Bobby is putting.
(Photo by George Pietzcker)

The two Bobbys: Cruickshank and Jones.

Right to left: Bobby Jones, Bobby Cruickshank, Laurie Ayton, Walter Hagen, Al Espinosa, Tommy Armour, Clarence Hackney, and Dave McKay. (Photo from Getty Images)

Bobby and Tommy Armour cooling off after a round.
(Photo by George Pietzcker)

Bobby and Al Espinosa waiting to tee off.

Nellie, Estelle Armour, and Jo Espinosa: the three wives who are credited with the idea of starting an organized golf tour. They wrote to chambers of commerce to set up tournaments in a logical order so the pros did not have to retrace steps.

Tommy Armour and "The Black Hawk," the car the Armours and Cruickshanks used to travel to the tournaments on the West Coast in the winter of 1927–1928. (Photo from the USGA)

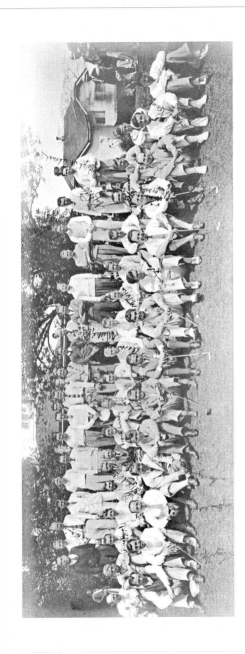

The First Master's field in 1934 at Augusta National.
(Photo permission from Augusta National)

*Bobby and Gene Sarazen at the 1934 US Open at Merion Golf Club.
Bobby literally knocked himself out of contention on the eleventh
hole of the final round. He finished third. (Photo from the AP)*

Bobby and Sam Snead at the 1937 US Open at Oakland Hills.
(Photo from the AP)

Elsie, Nellie, and Bobby returning from the British Open in 1937.

*Bobby receives the 1943 North and South medal from Donald Ross.
Looking on are Joe Kirkwood and Joe Turnesa. (Photo from the AP)*

1926 and the Ten-Inch Putt

The first group of pros in the Metropolitan area to leave on December 7, 1925, included Bobby, Cyril Walker, Johnny Golden, Danny Williams, and John O'Connor. They planned to meet up with the Chicago-area pros, who included Mike Brady and Tommy Armour, to begin their quest with the $5,000 Monterrey Peninsula Open.

In 1926, Bobby had gotten the tags of "second-place pansy" and "Joe Hard Luck" for his near misses. In the winter of 1926, he was second at Los Angeles, second in Texas, lost a playoff at Hot Springs, and a playoff in the Florida Open, and he was third and fourth in other tournaments. At the North and South he decided he had been playing too safely and vowed to play every shot to the max. At last, he broke through to win the North and South. Friends said he was just waiting for "the big one." Before the Masters, the North and South at Pinehurst was considered a major along with the Western Open.

However, it was his second-place finish at the Texas Open that caused a controversy debated across the country for a year.

The controversy took place in the last round of the Texas Open at the Brackenridge Golf Club in San Antonio in February. Bobby was a shot ahead of MacDonald Smith coming to the last hole. Smith played the hole perfectly, but Bobby ran into trouble after hooking his tee shot. He arrived at the eighteenth green needing to sink a twenty-foot putt to win the tournament, or at least a two putt for a playoff and a chance. The Texas Open meant a lot to the young golfer, as it would be his biggest win.

The gallery at the Texas Open was restless and inexperienced in watching tournaments. Since 1923, local newspapers wrote articles about proper behavior while watching golf, as the state wanted to be known for having the best galleries in the country. One piece of advice was to think of ropes as barbed wire and don't argue with marshals. Don't count up the score loudly when a golfer is ready to putt to see what score he would make if he sank it. Don't stand in the bunkers and don't walk in front of the players when they are ready to hit a shot. Joe Williams wrote in 1924, "Ropes, Boy Scouts, and prayers make up the main ingredients of the system now in use."

Remaining still and quiet when a player was making a shot was not the usual behavior when watching a sporting event, so Bobby asked Big Bill Furlough, the head marshal, to quiet everyone down. Big Bill walked out onto the green with a megaphone and said that no one should move or make any noise when the players putted.

Some in the gallery perched in trees behind the hole so they could see the finish. One of those was fellow competitor, Wild Bill Mehlhorn. He was not in contention and had finished his round but wanted to see the final hole between Wee Bobby and Mac Smith.

Bobby lined up his putt to win, but he came up ten inches short, a virtual gimme to tie and force a playoff. Just as he struck the short putt, an ear-splitting yell pierced the air that startled Bobby to the point he missed the putt, thus losing the tournament and any chance at the first prize. The story of the missed putt and the yell went 'round the country from Oakland, California, to New York City. It would start a controversy hotly disputed for over a year.

Opinions vary from exactly what happened to the size of the putt. Bobby heard that Wild Bill fell out of the tree at the moment of the putt. Bobby believed this story. However, the next day headlines screamed: "Mehlhorn Very Rude to Bobby! Costs Him the Title."

Like the children's game of telephone, the story morphed from one explanation to another. Bobby became the "whispering Scot" and Mehlhorn was known as "Machinery Bill," since one version of what happened involved a delivery truck. The driver, in one version, had left his motor idling when he went into the clubhouse. Jack O'Brien, the tournament's founder, went over to turn off the motor. Mehlhorn, perched in the tree, yelled over, "What do you know about machinery!" just at the wrong time.

Another version had "Wild Bill" reporting from the tree to those underneath who couldn't see the green.

Everyone weighed in. Sports fans from other sports could not understand why golfers were so upset about noise. Fellow players weighed in. Al Espinosa said that Mehlhorn was known for that sort of thing. He said that Mehlhorn called him names before the gallery at the PGA tournament, and even his wife spoke to Mehlhorn about it, but he wouldn't listen. It might be noted that the Espinosas were best friends with Bobby and Nellie. Mehlhorn's manager said that Mehlhorn didn't know his voice would carry.

Jimmy Powers wrote a year later that Mehlhorn perched in a tree and "gave a first-class imitation of an Alpine yodeler that caused Cruickshank to miss a three-inch putt."

Not everyone was on Bobby's side. In the *Joplin News* editorial, a writer said: "That was Bobby's fault absolutely. And Bobby is playing the poorest role in sportsmanship when he lays it on Bill. An alibi is a sickly thing." The editor went on to say that many great people had "alibis," like Demosthenes, who had a stutter but still became a great orator. The editor said that Demosthenes would not have let the yell bother him and would not have missed the putt if he had been playing in the tournament.

Writer Westbrook Pegler wrote, "Cruickshank, who is notoriously touchy about the sound of rustling leaves or the twitting of birds," searched the trees for Bill Mehlhorn when he heard the sound of a machine.

Will Rogers got in on the act, writing a piece called "What America Needs Is Better Putters." He found the quiet needed by golfers amusing. He said that "just the rustle of the five spot from a lone mate caused Bobby Cruickshank to miss an eight-inch putt."

Bobby always believed it was Mehlhorn who might have had a few *brews* after the tournament and subsequently fell out of the tree. The *New York Times* reported the incident right after it happened and stated that Mehlhorn tried to apologize, but Bobby would not accept it. The disappointment was huge for Bobby so early in his career, but in an article, Bobby said that although he was disturbed, it was without question his fault that he missed the putt.

The incident is now part of Texas Open lore and some say a whisper on the eighteenth hole became a shout over time. Bobby always insisted it was an ear-piercing yell.

A few weeks after the incident, Bobby and Mehlhorn met in a playoff at the South Central in Arkansas. The press loved it. Bobby lost to Mehlhorn, but they showed no animosity, and Bobby warmly congratulated him on the win and meant it. Bobby did not hold grudges and absolutely knew the yell was not intentional.

The following year, Bobby returned and won the Texas Open, playing with Mehlhorn in the final round. Time heals even a breach of proper golf behavior, especially when followed by a win.

Wild Bill had one more misunderstanding with Bobby. Always searching for the secret of putting, Bobby decided that he should close his eyes when he hit his putt. He and Wild Bill were paired together, and things were going very well for Bobby, who was sinking every putt and led the tournament when he arrived at the ninth hole. Convinced he had found the secret, Bobby saw Jimmy Donaldson, a dapper golfer, with his camel-hair jacket draped over his shoulders and a cigarette in a long holder. Bobby walked over and said, "Jimmy, watch this. I've found the secret to putting."

He went to his putt and proceeded to stub his putter behind his ball, literally whiffing it.

Donaldson flicked his cigarette and said, "Lovely style, Robert," as he turned and walked away.

Bobby was so angry he said he "could have burst."

Wild Bill thought Bobby blamed him again, which was not the case, but some in the gallery thought so, too, and booed Bobby.

In 1931, Bobby and Wild Bill did an exhibition tour together in the Far East, and they got along well. Was Wild Bill rude? Did Bobby have rabbit ears? Eventually, golf moved on.

Travel: Touring in the Twenties and Thirties

Travel proved to be an adventure for the pros touring in the twenties and thirties. Passenger travel by air didn't exist. Car travelers had to deal with poor roads, finding places to eat, and stay, as well as locating gas when needed. Train travel provided the transportation method of choice. However, train schedules often could not be counted on to be reliable. Once, on the way from Texas to the South Central in Hot Springs, the pros had to disembark the train to wait for another, which would arrive in about three hours. Unfortunately, there was no station where they had to disembark, only an unoccupied hut. Nellie remembered that all they could see was desert.

As night fell, Bobby swore he heard a "bloody cougar" not too far away. The pros piled up the steamer trunks to make tables. Out came the cards, where money changed hands in the moonlight. Nellie claimed that they had as much fun on that trip as any she can remember. The train arrived a few hours later to take them to Hot Springs.

In the beginning of December, Nellie got the urge to pack up and get going as much as the pros did. She had to pack for a trip of almost five months, with clothes for every type of weather and for every occasion—from golf to galas. There was no going back once they started off, because traveling to California was not only costly, but a three-day trip on the train. She also packed Elsie's toy chest with her favorite toys, leaving room for treasures picked up along the way—a rock from the desert or a new doll.

Bobby packed his clubs as well as extra shafts, grips, and heads, since no overnight shipping existed to replace broken equipment—wooden clubs snapped easily. Also, porters could be rough on the clubs or leave them near the heater in a baggage car. The pros had to know about club making and repair. Often the first stop was the golf shop at the tournament site, where the vise was a golfer's best friend. Bobby and Leo Diegel probably spent more time than anyone else fiddling with their clubs—straightening the lie one day, flattening it the next.

Nellie took great pride in how good they looked. After all, the pros were putting on a show, grateful for the fancy clubs that agreed to hold a tournament. They were responsible for promoting the tournaments. Bobby had his well-pressed plus fours, stockings, a crisp shirt, and tie. Sometimes that meant turning over a bureau drawer in the hotel room for Nellie to iron the clothes. Sending clothes out for quick cleaning wasn't possible.

Leo Diegel, who took great pride in how he looked, was also superstitious. One time he led a tournament but got soaking wet in a rainstorm on the course. He wanted to wear his lucky outfit the next day. The hotel staff worked through the night to see his clothes were dry and pressed, even managing to dry his shoes. He happily donned his lucky clothes the next morning. Unfortunately, he shot in the eighties.

The journey west started off in early December. The pros in the Metropolitan area took the Twentieth Century Limited for the trip to Chicago.

This train, with its art deco décor, on-time record, and other amenities, was a top choice for travel. A red carpet laid out in Grand Central for passengers to board and disembark added to the image of luxury. News photographers regularly appeared at the station in case there were celebrities getting on or off—the first paparazzi.

The pros stayed in the same car and slept in berths covered by curtains. An upper berth cost $18.60, with the more expensive lower ones at $32.70. Travelers could enjoy excellent dining, a club car, and an observation car on a trip with few stops. In twenty hours, they pulled into Chicago, where everyone going to Los

Angeles changed trains. The Midwest pros joined the group for the sixty-three-hour ride on the all-Pullman Santa Fe Chief across the country.

Nothing was too good for the passengers on the Santa Fe Chief: fine dining, the club and observation cars, maids, valets, and a barbershop, but no showers. Air conditioning didn't exist, and open windows brought in grime and dirt. Regardless of these discomforts, the pros had fun. They played gin rummy, told stories, caught up, made plans, and had putting contests in the aisle. Nellie often spoke of the closeness of the golfers. She attributes this in large part to the hours they spent together. They had to rely on each other to make travel plans and find places to stay, as they had no agents or managers to help. At a site they stayed in the same hotel, ate together, and spent their leisure time together.

For years, Elsie was the only child following the tour, and she was in heaven. Her upper berth was her private cave and she easily fell asleep to the steel-on-steel lullaby of the rails. At tournaments she thought the clubhouses were her castles, where servants brought her sweets and cool drinks. She got more attention than a flea on a dog from the pros and their wives, and she loved having a train full of doting "aunts and uncles" who read to her and played games. She retrieved the balls in the putting contests in the aisles when she was old enough. She made chiffon and lace hankies for her favorite golfers, which they all wore in their jacket pockets when she was looking, to the surprise of onlookers. The pros did not want to hurt her feelings, and they knew she kept tabs. When her toy chest was accidentally put off the train at a stop, the pros hounded the station until it was returned. Nellie said, "They were just as interested in that toy chest as we were. They were Elsie's family."

Elsie enjoyed walking nine holes, and Nellie told her made-up stories as they walked. Estelle Armour said she was always amazed that a reporter could come up to Nellie and ask how the players were doing. She could rattle off hole by hole scores and immediately continue on, "And then the little bunny . . ."

When Elsie was six, Nellie had to buy her a full fare ticket. Expenses were always a consideration, and Mabel Walsh once said, "Elsie's so small, why don't you just say she's five?"

Nellie taught Elsie to read early, which was all well and good until the conductor stopped by as Elsie was reading.

"My, aren't you a smart young lady. How old are you?" he asked.

"I'm five and a half on the train, but I'm six when I'm not," Elsie answered. An embarrassed Nellie bought a full-price ticket.

When the pros rolled into the Union Passenger Terminal in Los Angeles, they had tried to spruce up as best they could to meet the press, who were always waiting.

Nellie remembered they could usually work out of Los Angeles for a few weeks. Movie star golf fans abounded, and the pros enjoyed the hospitality offered by such stars as Douglas Fairbanks and his wife, Mary Pickford. They welcomed the pros and their wives to their estate, Pickfair, with its large pool and servants to tend to refreshments.

Golf enthusiasts Harold Lloyd and Charlie Chaplin enjoyed Bobby's company; he was a great mimic. Tommy Armour said Bobby had them in stitches at parties as he showed how he thought various actors would swing a club. In fact, Henry Cotton said later that Bobby and Tommy "knew all the tricks. Two cross-talk comedians would find it hard to keep up with these first-class kidders."

Harold Lloyd was a good golfer and had a nine-hole course with nineteen water hazards on his Beverly Hills estate. He hosted the golfers and he had a fun tournament there for the pros when it was possible with his schedule.

During the down time between tournaments, there were a lot of matches where money changed hands. Bobby and Tommy were a successful team. Tommy handled the negotiations and or-dered Bobby to stay out of the deal-making. Bobby said he often sank down in his seat as Tommy arranged the bets. For instance, the opposing team would play their best ball against Tommy and

Bobby's worst ball. Tommy was a savvy arranger, and they usually came out on top.

The pros not only stayed at the same hotel but tried to stay on the same floor when possible. They could easily visit with one another. One time at Pinehurst, Elsie slept on the screened porch off her parents' room. She awoke to hear one of the pros wooing a lady under her room in the moonlight.

"I love you with all my thumping, bumping heart," he opined.

Elsie roused her parents, who went up and down the hall waking their friends. Like teenagers at a pajama party, they all crammed into Nellie and Bobby's room to hear the ardent pro whom they all knew. The next day it was hard to keep a straight face when they saw him.

The pros and their wives in their free time went to a movie or attended the American Legion fights in Los Angeles. If not too tired, some went dancing. Nellie said the best dancers were Joan and Paul Runyan, Mabel and Frank Walsh, and Vi and Jimmy Thompson.

Nellie also claimed that stories about heavy drinking during the tournaments were not true and would argue the point with anyone. During the tournaments Nellie vowed the pros took care of themselves. Expenses were high, and they were paying their own way. Also, tournaments were played in seventy-two holes over Saturday and Sunday, which demanded being in good physical shape. If a pro's tee time was nine a.m., he expected to finish by twelve, which gave him an hour for lunch to make his one o'clock second-round tee time. Sometimes lunchtime might have been thirty to forty-five minutes, but mostly they had an hour.

The pros had to be their own promoters of the tournaments. They appreciated that the members gave up their course for the event. Jo Espinosa always wrote a thank-you letter saying she and Al liked it so much that when he retired, they would come back there to live.

Nellie said, "Jo, you know you don't mean that."

"But it makes them feel so good," Jo said.

Bobby knew the members were proud of their course. He made a point of finding something nice to say even if it was to point out a beautiful tree.

If possible, the pros tried to arrange exhibitions between tournaments to help with expenses. Bobby and Tommy played many exhibitions together. One time after a tournament in Portland, they arranged exhibitions in Seattle and Tacoma. Nellie and Estelle planned to stay in Portland, where they would all meet up to travel back down to California.

The wives waited, but when their husbands didn't arrive in time for the train, they decided to board and hope their mates would join them somewhere along the line.

Meanwhile, Bobby and Tommy had been invited to a party after the exhibition in Tacoma. They thought it would be fun, but lost track of time and realized they had missed the train. According to Bobby, they hired a car to rush them over the mountain to catch the train, not asking about the cost. When they arrived at the station, the driver said it would cost $150. Bobby called it highway robbery, but what could they do? It took most of the exhibition money.

"What will we say to the girls?" Bobby asked.

"We'll bluff it out, get on the club car, and demand to know where they've been."

"What about the money?"

"Poor gate," said Tommy.

Nellie did not see them until the next morning, when she heard a Scotch brogue behind a curtain, "Porter, bring me some coffee."

It was a silent ride back to California with little money to show for their efforts.

One problem traveling by train was that tournaments ended on Sunday. The pros were often paid in cash. They could not get to a bank to wire the money back to their own banks until Monday. Rumor had it there were robberies on the trains, so the wives used to pin the winnings in their bras for safekeeping.

Nellie said a person could see how well a golfer did by the expansion or contraction of his wife's bosom.

One might think that a car would make life easier, but Nellie disagreed. After winning the US Open in 1927, Tommy received a big black Stutz Bearcat that they named the Black Hawk.

"How I hated that car," Nellie said. "It caused more trouble than it was worth. The exterior was grained leather. You can imagine the dirt of the desert settling into it. The very delicate window cords had a tricky opening and closing system. This meant that half the time we were driving with rain pouring in or freezing to death."

On one trip, the car just stopped dead in the middle of nowhere. They were going from San Francisco to San Jose. Tommy and Bobby knew nothing about cars. Tommy's mechanical ability, according to Nellie, ended with kicking the tires. Eventually, another car came by. The driver recognized the golfers and offered them a lift to the course at San Jose.

Off they went with a shout, "We'll send help." Nellie and Estelle didn't know what to expect as they sat in the car on the side of the road. Apparently, Tommy did call a repair service when he arrived at the course, and a truck came at last. The mechanic made one small adjustment. Fortunately, Estelle, unlike Nellie, could drive and off they went arriving at the end of the round.

"I was so glad when Tommy got rid of that car in the spring," Nellie said.

Sadly, for Nellie and Bobby, the time came when Elsie was about nine that a wrenching decision had to be made. In those days homeschooling wasn't an option, and Nellie and Bobby were informed that Elsie, even though her grades were always good, could not miss the months they spent away. They could go to jail. Elsie felt that she learned a lot more traveling around the country than she ever learned in school. Her parents and her Aunt Jo Espinosa made sure she saw all the sights. Luckily, the Smiths in New Jersey were like family and were happy to have Elsie stay with them during the western tour. "Smithie" became her second mom. Elsie said she never had a problem with this arrangement, as she said she was proud of her father and his golf. On the occasion when she had been naughty and had to be punished, Elsie would inform Smithie that she was going to California to be with her parents. Smithie would say, "That's fine, dear. You go two blocks to the streetcar and when you get to Orange, get on the train to Newark. Then change for New York. When you get there, go to the other station and there you'll find the train to Los Angeles." That always ended it.

Elsie said that life is only strange to those who don't live it. She remembers the times fondly. Sometimes the most difficult things spur the happiest of memories. Travel was definitely an adventure, and the little band of barnstormers drew close and formed lifelong friendships.

In the meantime, the tour was growing quickly, and 1927 would turn out to be Bobby's best year.

The Best Year: 1927

The year 1927 was the thirty-first year for golfers in the United States. Ray McCarthy reported there were two thousand golf and country clubs and two million golfers. People were buying golf equipment and golf clothes. The automobile proved to be an impetus for the growth of golf, enabling people to get to the courses.

With the increasing money offered, the pros again eagerly boarded the train in December 1926, to embark on the quest for riches. Still, with no sponsors and high costs, pros often partnered up to split purses. In 1926–1927, Bobby teamed up with Johnny Golden. Bobby was to have his best year in professional golf.

He started his banner year winning the Los Angeles Open with its first prize of $3,500. The Los Angeles Open, for the first time, charged a fee for the spectators. Officials worried that people might not be willing to pay one dollar per day to watch, but the size of the gallery did not decrease. Bobby won by six shots.

Then it was on to the Texas Open. Prior to that tournament Bobby and Tommy arranged to play in an exhibition there. They usually played for the gate. When they got to the site they saw a course with little grass, sand greens, and oil derricks rising from the ground like giant trees. There was one lone man.

"What will we do?" asked Bobby.

"We have to play," Tommy said. "We've given our word."

The gentleman followed quietly along, and Bobby and Tommy did their best. At the end, the man pulled out a wad of bills and counted out as much as they would have received at a successful exhibition. He was a wealthy oil baron and had wanted to see them play.

The Texas Open also decided to charge to watch the event. Tickets cost fifty cents. The spectators parked a half mile away, so the club provided buses to run every half hour starting at 5:45 a.m. at a charge of fifteen cents. The galleries also did not shrink because of the cost.

After the infamous ten-inch putt of 1926, Bobby, paired with Wild Bill, went on to win the Texas Open easily without incident. However, a report said he lost two shots when he was bothered by a movie camera.

Then it was on to Hot Springs and the South Central. In cold, rainy weather Bobby added another win. He finished third at Shreveport and second in the Florida Open. Bobby and Tommy teamed up to win the International Four Ball in Miami, beating Gene Sarazen and Walter Hagen nine and eight in the thirty-six-hole final.

Meanwhile, Johnny Golden was having a lackluster tournament season. He came to Bobby and said he didn't think it was fair he had contributed so little, and they should cancel the agreement. Bobby didn't want to, because he felt an agreement was an agreement. He was not concerned about splitting the purses, but Golden insisted.

At the next tournament, the Southern Open, the purse was $12,000, Tournaments had started trying to outdo each other in prize money. Bobby Jones was in the field and the galleries were huge. Just prior to the Southern Open Bobby joined up with amateur Jess Sweetster to play an exhibition against amateur Bobby Jones and Walter Hagen. Bobby and Sweetster won with a best ball of sixty-four to Jones and Hagen's sixty-seven. As expected, Jones went on to win the tournament. As an amateur, he could not take the prize money. Johnny Golden had found his game and tied for the first prize money. He played off. On the last playoff hole, Golden was a shot ahead. He went to his drive and found it rolled into a popcorn box, and he couldn't see the ball. He decided to take a blind whack at it, and to his surprise, it ended up on the green. He won the playoff. Bobby rushed up to congratulate him, laughing that he picked a good time to dissolve the partnership. Golden said, "What do you mean? We had a deal, and if you had won I'd have sued you for the money." Bobby did not want to take half, but Golden insisted.

Next, it was on to Pinehurst for the North and South. Bobby was defending champion, and most people did not think he'd repeat. Joe Kirkwood disagreed and bought Bobby in the calcutta. In a calcutta, a person chooses the player he believes will win. If he has the highest bid, he wins the pot. Bobby did defend successfully, and Joe won a goodly sum.

That summer, Tommy won the US Open at Oakmont. When Nellie heard some people making snide comments about the high winning score, she was indignant. With no wedge, the pros had to get out of the many bunkers with only a niblick. The bunkers were raked into deep furrows, which made the shot especially difficult.

Bobby was still a British citizen when he traveled to the Canadian Open that summer. He realized he forgot his papers to get back in the country. Panicked, he said to his fellow travelers on the train, "What will I do?"

Mabel Walsh, wife of Frank said, "Just say you were born in the USA."

Bobby was a terrible liar. When the customs official asked where he was born, Bobby answered in his thick Scottish brogue where he lived. Unfortunately, he lived in Por-r-r-r-r-rt Chester-r-r-r. The customs official laughed so hard he waved him through.

Along with the tournaments, Bobby and Tommy played more exhibitions, which added to the coffers. They beat Sarazen and Hagen again at an exhibition at Congressional, where Tommy was pro.

Bobby wrote a series of golf articles for the newspaper, which advertised him as the man who beat Hagen, Farrel, Sarazen, Diegel, Cooper, and Mehlhorn. The paper bragged Bobby took careful pains with the articles, being sure he had the exact picture he wanted to show the swing. It said that a private lesson with Bobby would cost twenty-five to fifty dollars.

In an interview, Bobby had one more piece of free advice when a reporter asked him how to stop topping the ball. Bobby replied it was easy, "Just turn the ball over and hit it on the bottom."

Golf writer Jimmy Powers stopped calling Bobby a "second-place pansy" and started recognizing his small size at five foot four and jolly nature, calling him "the bouncing barrister" or "a pint-sized thistle," or "gallant god of the shrimps." Ed Sullivan called him a "midget star." Arthur Daley later said, "A little fellow in stature was Bobby Cruickshank but he was a big man in golf."

It was during the winter of 1926–1927 that Nellie, Estelle Armour, and Jo Espinosa decided there should be some order to the tour. Sometimes when tournaments just popped up, they had to retrace steps, which added to expenses. The wives decided to write to the Chambers of Commerce to say how their city would benefit if they sponsored a tournament. They hoped to fill up the schedule so there was not as much downtime. They were pleasantly surprised at the positive responses they received, and this provided a chance for tournaments to be set up in a logical order. They also wrote to hotels suggesting that the pros should receive special rates for staying there, which they got. They were very aware how the golfers had to also be the promoters. Ben Hogan said the wives started the concept of a tour. "Before that you had just a smattering of tournaments across the country. The wives kept up the correspondence and handled the books. Then the manufacturers saw what a great promotional vehicle the tour could be and hired Bob Harlow . . . Later the PGA got in on it."

In the 1928–1929 tournament year, Tommy, Bobby, and some other pros formed the American Tournament Golfers' Association. Tommy Armour was named president. Hal Sharkey, a golf writer, was appointed secretary-treasurer. Bobby and Al Espinosa were on the board. The group sanctioned the dates for the tournaments.

Their three wives, along with Mrs. Mac Smith, followed their husbands every round in good weather and bad. The only place where Nellie sometimes didn't follow was Texas, because when it was damp, the red clay stuck on the soles of shoes. Golfers had to carry screwdrivers to chip it off every couple of holes.

Nellie had a good eye for problems that might creep into Bobby's swing. In between rounds, if he had some trouble, she would tell him, for example, "Your head is not steady on your putts.

He would say, "You don't know what you're bloody talking about." But she would see him trying it out, and he would always come back and thank her. She always sat right behind the pin on the par threes so he would have something to aim at. She made a point of keeping his spirits up by saying there would always be a next time.

Jo Espinosa also tried to offer encouragement. She made Al recite every morning, "Every day in every way I am getting better and better and better."

In one tournament, Bobby and Tommy were paired with Mike Brady. They were playing well and sinking putts, but Mike was having a terrible putting day. Estelle and Nellie felt so bad for Mike's wife, Gracie, they told her that Bobby and Tommy had started a milk diet at lunch instead of coffee and it was helping. So Gracie suggested to Mike he ought to try milk at lunch. On the first hole of the afternoon he missed another short putt. In a loud voice he yelled, "Gracie, you and your damned milk diet!" Gracie was embarrassed, but the gallery loved it. Because there were no ropes, the gallery could always be up close to the golfers and never miss a thing.

Horton Smith recognized Nellie, Estelle Armor, Jo Espinosa, and Mrs. Macdonald Smith as being great assets to their husbands and were able to see faults that crept into their swings. He felt the wives were responsible for their husbands getting good jobs. Bobby told him he always felt better when Nellie was with him at a tournament.

Nellie knew that the tension could make tempers flare. She took care to check how a golfer was doing before saying anything. "We had to have a sense of humor about the shenanigans of our husbands," she said.

The sandy lies in the Florida rough tested a lot of golfers. After much searching, Jo Espinosa found a dapper Panama hat for Al, and she was so pleased with how he looked. Alas, one bad shot too many from a sandy lie caused him to take off his hat and proceed to jump up and down on it, leaving it in tatters.

Florida was the only place Nellie ever saw the usually even-tempered Mac Smith lose it. She saw him snap his club in two after a shot out of a sandy lie. Harry Cooper threw his driver so high up it lodged in a tree. She saw Tommy get so mad that he completely buried his putter in the bunker yelling, "You'll never make me miss another putt!" She wondered how Bobby had a foot left after slamming himself with a putter on the toe of his shoe after a mistake.

Nellie said, "I've hidden behind bushes and laughed heartily at the little displays."

Not everyone admired the wives. Gene Sarazen said in an article that wives shouldn't be out there following their husbands. He saw too many mad faces when the poor golfer missed a putt he should have made.

Nellie loved Gene and didn't pay any attention to him. In fact, she agreed with him in many cases. She said, "I have watched the expressions on some of the wives and thought to myself that if their poor husbands got a glimpse of what I saw, it wouldn't be helpful. I saw a young wife kick her husband in the shins, because she knew he could do better, but she didn't know this elusive game of golf."

1928–1930 and the Big Bet

Golf was riding high. Tournament money for the winter continued to grow. Bobby prepared to defend his many titles from the year before. He was third in Nassau, third in the Texas Open, and third in the Florida Open. He and Tommy were runners-up in defending the International Four Ball in Miami. It was only the second loss in team play for Bobby and Tommy. Sarazen and Farrell beat them two and one in the thirty-six-hole final. La Gorce offered a $15,000 purse, which was matched by the Southern Open.

At La Gorce, Bobby led on the last day. He went out in thirty in the afternoon of the final round and felt he had the tournament won. He chose to play cautiously on the back nine and shot par thirty-six. However, Johnny Farrell, out after him, matched Bobby's thirty and came in with thirty-three, so Bobby again finished second. Bobby said he made a mistake playing safe golf. He said if you're a stroke back or a stroke ahead, you know how to proceed—you shoot the works. But with a big lead you tend to play for pars and you're lucky to keep the lead. He said, "It is a savage business setting the pace." He vowed not to do that again.

At the end of the winter of 1928, Johnny Farrell and Mac Smith led the money list with $4,500 each. Bobby won $4,300.

In 1928, some were still concerned about money intruding into golf. Top amateurs like Jess Sweetster, George Von Elm, and Glenna Collette received cars from their proud clubs. Bobby Jones received a house worth $50,000. He returned it saying it did not look good for him as an amateur to take such a gift.

In the spring of 1928, Bobby won the Maryland Open with Tommy Armour in second. In the Richmond Open in April,

Bobby led after three rounds. In the fourth round he found himself in a lot of pain and shot an eighty-one. It turned out he had a double hernia and needed surgery. The operation kept him out of play from April until the end of July when newspapers reported he played his first round after his surgery at his home club on July 27 and had a hole in one. He had to miss the big tournaments that summer.

Johnny Farrell won the Open, beating Bobby Jones in an eighteen-hole playoff. The crowds were huge and unruly. Farrell was decades ahead of his time when he said it would be a good idea to rope off the fairways. He felt that would help not only the players but also the gallery to see better. Newspapers estimated Farrell's Open win would be worth $100,000 with endorsements and exhibitions.

Bobby's game in the fall had not gotten as sharp as he expected because of his time away from the game. He did go west, but he played poorly in the Los Angeles Open in January of 1929. He told people he wanted to turn in his card for a handicap. He said, "Holy E. Smokes. I'm so far off my game it will be season after next before I get started again as a beginner."

Purses continued to grow. Agua Caliente in Mexico offered the biggest purse ever: $25,000. Witt Bowman, Baron Long, and others financed the golf course at the resort. They wanted it to be so perfect for the tournament that no one could even practice on it. There literally was not one divot on the course when the pros teed off.

The winter of 1928–1929 offered purses totaling $125,000. By 1929 there were six thousand courses in the US. Indoor driving ranges had become popular. Golfers could now buy matched sets of clubs that were numbered so if a club broke, it could be replaced.

In 1929, six Bobby Cruickshank hickory shafted chrome plated irons sold for $26.50.

Factories churned out golf equipment. The Federal Trade Commission issued a complaint against the Spalding Company, which had started compensating pros who sold their clubs in their shops. The Commission said the members might be misled by the pros to buy Spalding, not knowing the pro would be earning money from the company for promoting their equipment. The Trade Commission also did not approve of the incentive to sell Spalding golf balls, because pros got free golf balls for so many sold.

In the winter of 1928–1929, Horton Smith was the new champion. Not yet twenty-one years old, he made $21,000 in prizes thanks to the $5,000 first prize at La Gorce.

Bobby tied with Bill Mehlhorn and Horton Smith at the South Central but lost the playoff to Mehlhorn.

Bobby and Tommy decided to return to Scotland in 1929 to visit family and play in the British Open. Bobby had not returned to Britain since he arrived in 1921. Sailing to Britain was a big commitment. Aside from the expense, the boat took at least a week to get there. The pro would have to be away from his club, so no lessons, and he would not be able to play in any of the tournaments or exhibitions in the States. In 1929, it was a Ryder Cup year, but Bobby and Tommy, not being native born, were not eligible. At this time no one thought that they might have played for Britain, as they had made their life in the states. Bobby left on February 24 for Britain. The Open was to be played at his favorite course, Muirfield. The *New York Times* quoted him saying, "I'm going to play a thousand rounds of golf. And the first day I get to Muirfield I'll play fourteen rounds."

Bobby and Tommy had arranged for an exhibition against the great English player Henry Cotton and his partner, Charles Whitcombe. The exhibition was for $1,250 a side, which Bobby and Tommy won. The British gallery did not know what to make of Cotton when he took a bag of balls out to practice. When Cotton had been in America, he observed the American pros on the range. Practicing and practice ranges were not part of British golf at that time, but Cotton thought it was a good idea. He shocked many golfers in Britain.

Nellie hired a car and driver and took the Ryder Cup wives on a tour of Scotland going west, into the lake district, over to St. Andrews, and back down to Edinburgh.

Bobby had to qualify at Gullane, which he did, just to get into the Open. Gale winds and icy rain greeted the golfers when the British Open began. Students from Bobby's old school, Daniel Stewart College, came out to watch him. Eager to help, they jostled each other to hold the umbrella for him, and Bobby got soaking wet. The wind blew so strongly, reports said Hagen's cigarette ashes blew back in his face, but Hagen won the Open with 292. Bobby was sixth at 301.

Nellie said she and Bobby usually met the British pros for a late cup of tea after dinner at tournaments. The talk always came back to Vardon, Ray, Duncan, and Mitchell. They would break up about 10:30 p.m. She felt the competitions in Britain were generally calmer than in the States.

Bobby returned to America in June and played in some tournaments, winning at Westchester. Farrell and Mike Turnesa were second.

Bobby won $500 in a driving contest. His three drives averaged 271 yards, with the longest at 283 yards with a driver almost as tall as he was. Farrell and Joe Turnesa finished second in the contest.

Bobby won the qualifying medal at the Metropolitan.

The pros looked forward to the winter with prizes of $25,000 at Agua Caliente, $10,000 at Los Angeles, and $15,000 at La Gorce and the Southern Open. Catalina was up to $7,500, and Hawaii was $6,000, as was Texas, who was trying to increase the purse.

Then October 1929 arrived, and the stock market plunged. However, the golf purses in the winter of 1929 and 1930 had not yet been greatly affected. Denny Shute won the Los Angeles Open with Bobby and Horton Smith tied for second winning $1312 each.

Bob Harlow had taken over running the tour. Pros started to be concerned about prize money, and pressured Harlow to push for guarantees. This attitude did not go over well with clubs, who said the pros better be careful or there would be no tournaments. In the 1929–1930 winter, Portland was off the calendar. Agua Caliente went from $25,000 to $15,000, and La Gorce was also reduced.

At the Savannah Open in the spring of 1930, Bobby was paired with Jones in the first round, shooting a sixty-nine to Jones's sixty-seven. He was so impressed with Jones's golf he asked O. B. Keeler what tournaments Jones was playing in that summer. Keeler said he was playing in the British Open and Amateur, and the US Open and Amateur. Bobby said, "He'll win them all." He sent fifty dollars to his father-in-law in Britain, who also put up fifty. They decided to parlay the bet. Jones, of course, went on to win the Grand Slam, and Bobby and his father-in-law split $10,700, which was very welcome, as the times were getting harder. Newspapers reported that Bobby won $107,000.

"I had a hell of a time explaining it to the IRS," Bobby said. He had to get an affidavit from the bookie in Britain.

Bobby was not in the US Open that year. When asked if he would have had any problems trying to win the Open with a bet on Jones, Bobby said he would give up ten times the prize for one US Open, which was true. The lack of an Open prize was his biggest disappointment in golf.

In the twenties and thirties, betting on tournaments was acceptable. Newspapers reported the odds on various players in a tournament. Clubs often held calcuttas, and at Los Angeles it was not uncommon for a player to go for a bid of $50,000. However, there were unsavory situations with bookies. At an amateur tournament at Oakmont, a bookie sent a fake telegram to a player, which said his father was dying before the golfer was to play a big match.

After his Grand Slam, Bobby Jones announced his retirement from golf in 1930. A reporter said it took Cruickshank three minutes before he could even speak about it. He knew it was a low for golf, as did the other players. Bobby said a tournament without Jones in the field would not be as great a win.

In 1930 things at Bobby's club, Progress, were dire. People could not pay for the merchandise they bought from him, which left Bobby with a huge debt, as he still owed the manufacturers. He was wiped out. It was not his nature to declare bankruptcy, so he wrote to the manufacturers and asked for time. They agreed and he ultimately paid off all he owed, even though it took a few years. The club was put up for sale, a far cry from the day in 1927 that the club awarded Bobby a $3,000 bonus for his fine play.

As golf grew in 1928–1929, equipment had flooded the market and prices dropped. Bobby's irons that used to sell for $6.50 now sold for $4.38. Sales at golf clubs that were still operating decreased. Exhibitions were harder to come by. People did not use their cars as much, and rounds of golf decreased. Some clubs went to daily fee courses. Winning the US Open was worth about half of what it used to be.

George Von Elm and Phil Perkins tried to form an association of Businessmen Golfers. They would be neither a pure amateur nor a pro. This venture did not succeed. Phil Perkins eventually turned pro.

Alan Hammond arranged for Bobby and Wild Bill Mehlhorn to embark on a Far East tour in the winter of 1930 into 1931. They would go to Honolulu, Japan, Manchuria, Hong Kong, and the Philippines. This offer came at a good time for Bobby, as times were tight and his club was no more. The purse for the Los Angeles Open had been reduced to $7,500. Agua Caliente was still $15,000, but La Gorce and Glendale were cancelled.

Bobby's first stop on the tour was Honolulu. He and Mehlhorn played two local players and won the match. In Japan, they were to help set up caddy training. The emperor, a golf enthusiast, arranged for Bobby and Wild Bill to stay in a home owned by the emperor's brother. Bobby and Wild Bill played exhibitions. The only match they lost was to the brothers Shiro Akaboshi and Rokura Akaboshi, who attended Princeton in the States and later designed courses in Japan. Bobby knew them from their time in the States. They were members of Shackamaxon when Bobby was pro there and had given them some lessons. He knew they were fine players.

In Manchuria, the war lord loved golf and was thrilled to follow. Then it was on to Hong Kong. Bobby was impressed with the Royal Hong Kong Golf Club and after their exhibition, he and Wild Bill wanted to give the caddies ten dollars. The British governor said no, and only let them pay the caddies fifty cents. In Shanghai, they played an exhibition in freezing weather on a course built inside a racetrack. In the Philippines, they enjoyed the largest galleries. During one match, Alan Hammond's false teeth bothered him. He took them out, and the caddies, who had never seen anything like this, dropped the bags and ran off.

Bobby was impressed with golf and golfers in the Far East and predicted the players there would make a success of golf in the West before long.

Bobby and Wild Bill played in some of the tournaments when they returned. The big money winner was Gene Sarazen with $8,332 in eight events. Bobby won $1,300 in the events he played in after returning from the Far East. With opportunities shrinking, money in golf would be even harder to come by as the Depression worsened.

Dire Times for Golf: 1931–1932

Bobby had a wife and daughter to support, so he was grateful to get a job at Port Richmond, a public course on Staten Island. Bobby had to ask permission to get time off to play in a tournament. Times were dire. The winter was fast approaching, and Bobby had to figure out some way to earn money. Unable to afford the trip west, he approached Macy's Department Store and proposed they would start an indoor golf school. They agreed, and Bobby taught there and sold golf equipment over the winter.

Many other pros did not go west for the 1931–1932 winter events. The pros who did not go west included Gene Sarazen, Walter Hagen, Johnny Farrell, Bill Mehlhorn, Denny Shute, Ed Dudley, Mac Smith, and Tommy Armour.

The Los Angeles Open now offered a purse of $5,000. They held the tournament at the Wilshire Country Club, which was nearer to town, hoping the gate would help with the purse. Long Beach wasn't held, and Pasadena and Santa Monica had purses of $2,500. Agua Caliente dropped to $7,500. In 1931, California only staged five tournaments.

With sales, lessons, and exhibitions decreasing, every tournament with any kind of purse was important. Gene Sarazen did the best at drawing galleries in the absence of Jones. Sarazen was still able to get exhibitions, and his club still paid him a good salary.

When pros did get exhibitions, they added lectures and instructions on how to play golf for the gallery. They were careful to play seriously so the gallery knew it was important. Sarazen and Tommy Armour played some exhibitions in which Sarazen taught the woods and Tommy the irons. Bobby played an exhibition in August of 1932 and was happy they had a gallery of 250. Bobby and Charles Mayo beat Wiffi Cox and Johnny Goodman one up.

Rounds of golf continued to decrease and dropped by 12 percent from 1930 to the beginning of 1932. People were not able to use their cars to travel out to the courses. However, Jimmy Powers reported that golf was doing better than other sports. Col. Jacob Ruppert, owner of the Yankees, said the days of high salaries were over. Babe Ruth's men's stores had to be sold to pay creditors.

In 1932, only three Americans went over for the British Open: Tommy Armour, who defended his win in 1931, Mac Smith, and Gene Sarazen, who won the Open in 1932.

The US Open in 1932 was held at Fresh Meadow in New York, Gene Sarazen's old course. The tournament still felt strange without Bobby Jones. Sarazen was the best hope for drawing large galleries. The pros were not sure he would play, but a cheer went up when he arrived. The USGA paired golfers up in ways to add interest for the gallery instead of drawing for pairings. Sarazen, who had just won the British, played with the defender, Billy Burke. Wiffi Cox was paired with Walter Hagen, as both loved galleries and enjoyed being jokesters. Bobby played with Jose Jurado, the Argentinian golfer who was a protegee of the Duke of Windsor. Both Bobby and Jurado were small men.

The USGA had considered playing the Open in four days instead of three, but that would be for a later time.

On Thursday, the opening day, the winds were high, and the scores generally matched the winds. However, Olin Dutra had a sixty-nine. Sarazen and Jurado had seventy-fours. Wiffi Cox shot eighty. Bobby had a seventy-eight, but he had an unusual start. His caddy was a young boy who had little experience. On the first hole, he held the pin when Bobby putted. Unfortunately, the caddy froze and couldn't remove the pin from the hole. Bobby's putt hit the pin and he incurred a two-shot penalty. The young boy was very upset, but Nellie said Bobby was more upset for the young boy than for the penalty, offering him consolation and encouragement. Who knows if that had an effect on the rest of his play that day?

Players never knew what experience a caddy might have.

Bobby would say when he got to a course, he hoped he would get a caddy who could tell him where the trouble was on the hole or if the greens held. With no yardage markers, a player had to eyeball what the distances were to the pins.

On Friday of the Open, Bobby had a seventy-four and started the last day seven back of Sarazen, the leader. Bobby's starting times were 7:45 and 11:55. Nellie stood with Grantland Rice and other reporters announcing she thought Bobby could still win, as he was playing well.

"They laughed at me," she said, "and set me to rights that no one comes from that far back. Well, he nearly did. In the morning round when I cut over from the eighth hole to the ninth, my friends were waiting for me. I think they knew the score as well as I did, as reports on very good or very bad rounds travel fast. I tried to look nonchalant and not over pleased. One asked me what Bobby was doing. I said, 'Two putts for a thirty-three.' They were nudging each other, all of them just as pleased as I was, because the press has always been very kind to Bobby."

At the end of the third round, Phil Perkins stood at 219, Sarazen and Jurado at 220, and Bobby at 221 after shooting a sixty-nine.

In the final, round Bobby came in with a sixty-eight. This was the first time a player in the Open had broken seventy twice in the double round. Phil Perkins came in with a tie, and Nellie thought there would be a playoff. However, Sarazen, in the final round, matched the all-time record set by Chick Evans, a sixty-six in 1916. Sarazen won by three shots. Sarazen's extraordinary performance meant another second place for Bobby in the Open. Sarazen became the only man besides Bobby Jones to win the US Open and the British Open in the same year. Papers reported that nine out of ten times Bobby's and Perkins's scores would have won, but a second place would have to do.

In 1932, Bobby made another great comeback. In the PGA, Bobby was playing Al Watrous. He found himself nine down with twelve holes to go. Bobby could look sad as a hungry puppy, and his unhappy bearing wasn't lost on Watrous.

Bobby said, "Al, this is the worst beating I ever had in my life."

Watrous, feeling sorry for him, gave him a tricky six-foot downhill putt. By some miracle Bobby caught fire. He won nine of the last twelve holes with a thirty-two on the back nine. Meanwhile Tommy was in the clubhouse bemoaning the fate of his friend.

He looked up and saw Bobby racing toward the first tee. "Where are you going, Cruicky?"

Bobby said, "I've tied it up and I'm going extra holes." He won on the forty-first hole, sinking a short putt. He lost to Frank Walsh the next day in the quarter-finals.

At the end of the year Bobby accepted the head pro job at the Country Club of Virginia, and after a difficult time, his life was on a more stable path as the Depression improved little by little.

1933-1937: Winding Down

Bobby played in the Open and PGA in 1933 but was not a factor in these tournaments. He was busy teaching at his new club. He did win the Virginia State Open. At a tournament at Charleston, South Carolina, Bobby went with one of his young pupils, Billy Howell. Bobby was leading after two rounds, but sadly Howell got word his mother passed away suddenly. Bobby immediately withdrew to accompany Howell back home. He did not consider doing anything else.

He did go out west for the 1933–1934 season. Bobby had a certificate from prizefighter Jeffrey Johnson's Barn, saying he boxed Denny Shute and won a three-round bout with a TKO in the second round. The Barn was the venue for amateur and professional boxing matches that were frequented by many celebrities. Bing Crosby was a big fan. Some of the golfers, when in the area, enjoyed attending. Whether this was a real bout or just a joke, no one knows, but Bobby and Denny Shute were boxers in school.

Bobby did win the Colonial Open in Nassau with a 267 (68-66-66-67), the Capital City Open in Washington, the Mid-South Scotch Foursome with Tommy, and a second straight Virginia State Open. At his home club he had twenty consecutive rounds under seventy and was ninety-three under par on the par seventy-two course. He had a sixty-five for a course record, four sixty-sixes, five sixty-sevens, seven sixty-eights, and three sixty-nines.

He played in the first Masters in 1934. In the early days the Masters was a low-key event with friends of Bobby Jones in the field. Pros and amateurs played and supported it, because of their high regard for Jones. There were many parties and some of the golfers enjoyed visiting a local nightclub for entertainment and dancing. Though the county was dry, liquor was available there.

At the 1935 Masters, Elsie was fourteen when she and a school chum joined her parents at the tournament, but were not allowed to go to the nightclub. A miffed Elsie hired a cab and she and her friend arrived at the club. When they entered, they attracted the interest of a patron who was slightly overserved. Walter Hagen and Grantland Rice saw this and spirited them off to the singer's dressing room, which meant an early night for Nellie and Bobby.

But it was the 1934 US Open at Merion at Philadelphia, for which he was remembered. Bobby played an exhibition in Richmond with Paul Runyan the Monday before the Open. At Merion he played his first two rounds in 71-71 and had a three-shot lead. After the third round, he was one back of Sarazen. The fourth round saw him take the lead again as he went to the back nine. In a twist of fate, the eleventh hole did Bobby in almost literally.

The eleventh was a short par four with a creek surrounding the green. Bobby only needed a mashie niblick for his shot. For some reason he laid off it a little, and his heart sank as he saw his ball fall into the creek. Then, a miracle! He saw the ball bound out of the water like a frightened duck onto the green. It had hit one of the flat rocks in the stream. Bobby thought that finally, luck was with him. He threw his club high in the air saying, "Thank you, God!" He charged forward, forgetting the club. Unfortunately, the club came crashing down on his head. Stunned, he fell to the ground. Blood poured out of the cut. For a moment everyone was silent, but Wiffi Cox had a situation he couldn't pass up. He went over and began counting Bobby out like a beaten prize fighter. Bobby staggered up.

He vowed to himself that he would finish no matter what. He did, but was five over on the last seven holes. The gallery had been so interested in the battle between Sarazen and Bobby that they overlooked Olin Dutra. Starting times on the last day were:

Bobby 10:25 and 2:25
Sarazen 10:50 and 2:50
Dutra was off last at 11:05 and 3:05

Dutra knew what he had to do and came in to win the Open. Sarazen finished second after a disastrous seven on number eleven, while Bobby and Wiffi Cox tied for third.

When Bobby came in, he received stitches on his head. He found Elsie sitting on the steps crying. He told her to be a good sport, that he accepted it, and so should she. Fate had intervened again. At thirty-nine Bobby believed this was in reality his last best shot. He moved on and had a funny tale to tell, but in truth, deep down, the blow from the club hurt more than he could say. Bobby's father-in-law visited from Scotland for the Open and knew what really happened. Filled with the superstition of a canny Scot, he swore he saw a black cat cross Bobby's path before the eleventh hole.

In the 1934–1935 winter events, Paul Runyan was the big winner with $6,787 in twenty-one events. Bobby earned $3,047.83 in eleven events. He beat Johnny Revolta in a playoff for the Orlando Open. He and Tommy were runners-up in defense of the Mid-South Scotch Foursome. He was second in the Miami Open and won the Virginia Open for the third time in a row.

He played some golf with Babe Didrikson. Some of the pros didn't want to be paired with her in a tournament, but Bobby and Tommy had no problem. In a tournament, on the first hole, which had a blind landing area, they teed off and walked to their drives. Bobby and Tommy stood aside when they got to the first ball.

Babe went over, checked the ball and said, "Mr. Armour, I think this is your ball." At the next ball, Bobby stood aside. When Babe checked, she said, "Mr. Cruickshank, this is your drive." She had outdriven them both. When asked by the press what Bobby thought about her prospects, he predicted greatness. He said she only needed experience to know when to gamble and when to play safe.

In 1936, Bobby and Nellie became American citizens. They had started the paperwork in 1929. Bobby was proud of this and said he wanted his entry in the Miami Open to say he was from Richmond, Virginia, USA.

At the Masters in the spring, Bobby shot a twenty-nine on the front nine in a practice round. He did not finish his round, because he didn't want to risk breaking Bobby Jones's course record. He went out later and had a seventy-two in his eighteen-hole practice round, ultimately finishing fourth in the tournament. He earned $450.

In the 1936 International Four Ball, Johnny Revolta and Henry Picard beat Bobby and Tommy in the semifinals, a rare defeat in that format. Bobby won his fourth straight Virginia Open.

The purses in tournaments had not yet achieved a level that made golf as valuable a sport as other games. Writer Henry M'Lemore said pros were basically playing for their own money considering entrance fees. Travel costs were high, and pros had not yet gotten lucrative merchandise contracts. From January to June, Horton Smith won Miami, Pasadena, and the Masters, but only earned $5,348. Gene Sarazen earned $2,818, Bobby $1,518, while Olin Dutra, Tommy Armour, and Johnny Farrell earned under a thousand.

Bobby had one more chance to win the Open in 1937. At Oakland Hills in Michigan Nellie once again thought Bobby might win at age forty-two. Oakland Hills was a tough tract with narrow fairways and high rough. Paul Runyan felt good about the course, because he was not a long hitter but was a straight one. He said to the newspapers he hoped the USGA would let the rough grow tall enough to hide Wee Bobby if he got in it. This tournament was twenty-four-year-old Sam Snead's first Open. He asked Bobby to look at his swing. Bobby said he had one of the best swings he had ever seen, and said he shouldn't change a thing. All he needed was experience, and Bobby rightly predicted greatness.

Bobby had picked the winner of the British Open, Henry Cotton, and he predicted Ralph Gudhal would win the US Open. Snead at twenty-four and Gudhal at twenty-five had been babies when Bobby was playing in tournaments. Snead and Bobby were the gallery favorites. In the third round Bobby came from no-where with a sixty-seven to put him in contention. The pundits had said that no one would break 290 on the difficult course. Bobby shot seventy-two in the final round and had the lead in the clubhouse at 285. Snead came in after Bobby with 283. The gallery thought he would win until Gudhal finished with a brilliant 281. Newspapers said all three deserved to win. Bobby won $700 for finishing third.

He won his fifth Virginia Open.

In 1938, Bobby accepted the head pro job at Gulf Stream Golf Club in Delray Beach, Florida, in the winter. He was still at the Country Club of Virginia in the summer. The winter trips to California were no more, but he happily spent his time teaching and playing in the occasional tournament. He left the Country Club of Virginia in 1947 to be pro in the summer at Chartiers Country Club outside of Pittsburgh. He stayed there for twenty happy years. Gulf Stream made him pro emeritus and let him retire in the pro's cottage where he had lived for thirty-seven years.

Afterword

Bobby spent his life playing the game he loved. He played golf on his days off from his clubs, and he stopped to play courses he accidentally found on his fishing trips. No course was too humble for him. He loved and admired his fellow players, and his philosophy was to never wish bad luck on your opponent—just try to do better. He never begrudged a fellow player winning.

When Bobby was in his seventies, shooting his age wasn't considered a good round. He liked to shoot under his age. At age seventy-seven he shot sixty-seven at Gulf Stream.

Bobby was elected into the original PGA Hall of Fame by the living Hall of Fame members. Tommy Armour said Bobby was "the luckiest unlucky golfer in the game . . . the lucky part was that he held the esteem and love of every player in the game and of every person he ever met . . . the unlucky side of his career was in the major golf championships. Great though his record is, with a little luck it could have been fabulous."

Arthur Daly, a *New York Times* columnist, wrote that before Arnie's Army there was Bobby's Brigade.

Bobby said, "Some say that I deserved some luck, but we had our chance. That's the way the Lord makes it, really. I have no regrets. I've loved it all my life. I think things work out for the best and if you win, you win, and if you don't, you don't. It's fate's work, you see."

When he couldn't play golf anymore, he quickly passed away. Hopefully, he is in his beloved Highlands with its braw hills that meant freedom. He is fishing in the salmon-filled Spey and playing games of golf in an eternal summer.

Golf Record

Edinburgh Coronation Trophy 1919, 1920
New York State Open 1921
St. Joseph, Missouri Open 1922
Spalding Tournament—Waykegal Golf Club 1922
Semifinals PGA 1922, 1923
Tied US Open—lost playoff to Bobby Jones 1923
Mid-Continent Open 1924
Colorado Open 1924
Fourth US Open 1924
Florida Golf League Winner with Johnny Farrell 1925
Oklahoma City Open 1925
North and South 1926, 1927, 1943
Tied Florida Open 1926
Mid-South Pro Am with George Voight 1926
Los Angeles Open 1927
Texas Open 1927
South Central Open, Hot Springs 1927, tied 1929
International Four-Ball with Tommy Armour 1927
Westchester 1927, 1929
Maryland Open 1928
US Open Runner-Up 1932
Virginia Open 1933, 1934, 1935, 1936, 1937, 1939
British Colonial Open, Nassau 1934
National Capital City Open 1934
Mid-South Scotch Foursome with Tommy Armour 1934
Orlando Open 1935
Third US Open 1937
Mid-Atlantic PGA Section Championship 1945
Tri-State PGA Championship 1949, 1950
Erie Open 1954
PGA Senior Stroke Play, Quarter Century, PGA Senior

Championship (at age seventy-seven shot six competitive rounds: 77-75-79-76-74-78. Won three age groups by forty-five strokes in 1972)

Elected to the Original PGA Hall of Fame 1967

Mid-Atlantic Hall of Fame 1996

Metropolitan PGA Hall of Fame 1976

Virginia Golf Hall of Fame 2019

Bobby's Rules of Life

Golf was life to Bobby. As his granddaughter, I often heard him explain his philosophy of right and wrong, of his aspirations, through the game of golf.

Be a good sport. In golf you will lose more than you will win, so you might as well learn to handle disappointment and move on.

Be pleasant even when your game is off. Don't make excuses.

Immediately shake hands with your opponent. Be sure you have a firm handshake.

Find something nice to say about the golf course you are playing. The members are proud of it and gave up their course at an inconvenience to them so you could play in the tournament.

Never wish ill will on an opponent. Play your own game and just try to do better.

Golf doesn't always work out the way you expect. One day you'll get bad bounces, but the next day you'll get some good ones. Things usually even out, so don't dwell on the negative.

Let your clubs do the talking.

You can't always be perfect. Some days you just have to play the game you brought to the course.

Make the best of things. If you bring a slice to the practice tee, plan to aim left.

Winning and losing takes place inside of you. If you worked hard and did your best, you might lose on the outside, but inside you know you are a winner. The only shame is to do less than your best.

Don't rest on your laurels. Nothing is certain. Keep going. If you are five up, get six up. If you are six up, get seven up. It isn't over until the last putt drops.

Bibliography

Most of the information is from oral and written history of Bobby Cruickshank, Nellie Cruickshank, and Elsie Cruickshank Hoke. The sources included below are to help verify the accuracy of the personal histories.

A special appreciation is given to Ross Goodner for the transcribed notes from extensive interviews of Bobby Cruickshank, which he sent to Elsie Cruickshank Hoke with the permission to use the information he acquired. Thanks to Wiffi Cox and Al Watrous, interviewed by author.

Associated Press. "Armour, Cruickshank Defeat Hagan, Sarazen." *Madison Wisconsin State Journal.* May 9, 1927. p. 9.

Associated Press. "Bobby Cruickshank Defeated by Hagen." *Salt Lake Telegram.* Salt Lake City, Utah. March 3, 1927. p. 5.

Associated Press. "Bobby Cruickshank Wins Annual Los Angeles Open Golf Tourney and $3500." *Monroe News Star.* Monroe, Louisiana. January 10, 1927. p. 7.

Associated Press. "Bobby Cruickshank Grabs Mid-Continent Golf Title." *Joplin Globe.* Joplin, Missouri. October 12, 1924. p. 9.

Associated Press. "British, American Golfers Play International Match." *Salt Lake Tribune.* Salt Lake City, Utah. March 21, 1929 p. 19.

Associated Press. "Cruickshank's 285 Adds Another Title." *Lowell Sun.* Lowell, Massachusetts. April 2, 1927. p. 24.

Associated Press. "Cruickshank and Armour Capture Four-Ball Title." *Albert Lea Evening Tribune.* Albert Lea, Minnesota. March 11, 1927. p. 11.

Associated Press. "Cruickshank and Voigt Winners Best Ball Event." *Sarasota Herald.* Sarasota, Florida. November 18, 1926. p. 8.

Associated Press. "Cruickshank Loses by One Stroke in Hot Springs Meet." *Mitchell Evening Republican.* Mitchell, South Dakota. February 5, 1926. p. 18.

Associated Press. "Cruickshank, Triumphant on Coast, Coming." *San Antonio Light.* San Antonio, Texas. January 10, 1927. p.10.

Associated Press. "Cruickshank Wins Maryland Title." *Hanover Evening Sun.* Hanover, Pennsylvania. October 1928. p. 3.

Associated Press. "Cruickshank Wins $1500 Texas Golf Open." *Joplin News Herald.* Joplin, Missouri. January 31, 1927. p. 8.

Associated Press. "Dallas Open Has Alluring Prizes." *San Antonio Express.* San Antonio, Texas. January 21, 1926. p. 12.

Associated Press. "Gene Sarazen Is the Big Money Winner of Winter Golfdom." *Daily Capital News.* Jefferson City, Missouri. April 2, 1931. p. 9.

Associated Press. "Golf Pros Form New Association to Aid Tourneys." *Oakland Tribune.* Oakland, California. December 31, 1927. p. 12.

Associated Press. "Horton Smith Tops Golf Money Winners." *Portsmouth Times.* New Hampshire. April 4, 1930. p. 22.

Associated Press. "Jones Leads at Savannah Open Golf Tournament." *Appleton Post Crescent.* Appleton, Wisconsin. February 21, 1930. p. 12.

Associated Press. "Made Big Winning on Bobby Jones." *Sedalia Capital.* Sedalia, Missouri. July 14, 1930. p. 16.

Associated Press. "Noisy Pro Cause of Golf Disaster for a Runner-Up." *High Point Enterprise.* High Point, North Carolina. January 18, 1926. p. 2.

Associated Press. "Open Golf Driving Tournament in East." *Bakersfield Californian.* Bakersfield, California. June 17, 1929. p. 6.

Associated Press. "Sarazen and Other Golfers Head West for Annual Meets." *Titusville Herald.* Titusville, Florida. p. 8.

Associated Press. "Sarazen Money Winner." *Daily Capital News.* Jefferson City, Missouri. April 2, 1931. p. 9.

Associated Press. "Smith Wins Texas Open Golf Meet." *Roswell Daily Record.* Roswell, New Mexico. January 18, 1926. p. 11.

Associated Press "Sports from the Sidelines." *Beatrice Daily Sun.* Beatrice, Nebraska. February 3, 1927. p. 6.

Associated Press. "Stroke Again Beats Golfer." *Hagerstown Daily Mail.* Hagerstown, Maryland. February 5, 1926. p. 10.

Beale, George H. "Money Cut Many Golf Pros Not Going West." *Sandusky Star Journal.* Sandusky, Ohio. December 21, 1932. p. 6.

Bell, Brian. "On the Sidelines." *Hagerstown Morning Herald.* Hagerstown, Maryland. July 26, 1930. p. 11.

Bell, Brian. Associated Press. "Who's Who in US Open." *Waterloo Evening Courier.* Waterloo, Iowa. June 26, 1929. p. 13.

Brown, Norman E. "Bobby Cruickshank as Joe Hard Luck." Central Press Sports ed. February 18, 1926. p. 8.

Burcky, Claire. "Glimpses of Golfers in the Open Tournament." *Kokomo Tribune.* Kokomo, Indiana. July 7, 1930. p. 10.

Carter, B. F. "Golf Precedes Ball 'in This Here League.'" *Winnipeg Tribune.* Alberta, Canada. July 31, 1924. p.18.

Conklin, Lee. International News Service. "Golfers Mourn Retirement of Bobby Jones." *Hammond Lake County Times.* Hammond Lake County, Indiana. November 18, 1930. p. 12.

Cruickshank, Bobby. "The Greatest Shot I Ever Saw." *Lethbridge Herald.* Lethbridge, Canada. September 3, 1925. p. 6.

Demaree, Al. "Goes Out of Bounds on 800 Acres." *Lawrence Journal World.* Lawrence, Kansas. November 10, 1927. p. 3.

Denny, Loren. Associated Press. "Par Succumbs as Pros Battle for Cash." *Wilson Daily News.* Wilson, North Carolina. p.13.

English, Tom. "The Little Big Man of Golf." *The Scotsman.* Edinburgh, Scotland. June 26, 2005.

Evans, Billy. "Billy Evans Says." *Logansport-Pharos Tribune.* Indiana. April 27, 1927. p. 9.

Farrell, Henry L. "Fanning with Farrell." *Piqua Daily Call.* Piqua, Ohio. February 2, 1926. p. 6.

Fullerton, Hugh. "Jones Realizes Life's Ambition." *Chicago Tribune Service.* Danville Bee, Virginia. July 16, 1923. p. 9.

Getty, Frank. "Speaking of Sport." *Valparaiso-Vidette Messenger.* Valparaiso, Indiana. July 6, 1929. p. 6.

Gould, Alan. Associated Press. "Smashing Finish Wins for Sarazen as Records Crash." *Kingsport Times.* Kingsport, Tennessee. p. 3.

Gill, Ted. Associated Press. "Richmond Pro Golf Winner." *Escambia Daily Press.* Escambia, Florida. December 21, 1934. p. 27.

Gram, Ralph. "Keeping Golf a Sport." *Davenport Democrat and Leader.* Davenport, Iowa. July 30, 1923. p. 6.

Horton, Chester. "Golf Lessons." *Lethbridge Herald.* Alberta, Canada. March 16, 1929. p. 3.

Keeler, O. B. "Cruickshank Champion Runner-Up." *Denton Record Chronicle.* Denton, Texas. April 10, 1928. p. 7.

Kilgallen, James. "Bad Six Months for Golf." *Dubuque Telegraph Herald.* Dubuque, Iowa. March 27, 1932. p. 14.

Krez, Art. "Golf by Art Krez." *Lubbock Morning Avalanche.* Lubbock, Texas. May 23, 1933. p. 4.

McCarthy, Ray. "Florida Team Golf a Failure." *Ogden Standard Examiner.* Ogden, Utah. February 15, 1925. p. 10.

Pegler, Westbrook. "Farrell and Cruickshank Finish in Tie in Florida Open Golf Tourney." *Sioux City Journal.* Sioux City, Iowa. February 28, 1926. p. 42.

Powers, Francis J. "US Winning Most Titles." *Sioux City Journal.* Sioux City, Iowa. July 24, 1927. p. 17.

Powers, Jimmy. "Georgian Gets Edge over Polished Field." *Ogden Standard Examiner.* Ogden, Utah. May 20, 1927. p. 33.

Powers, Jimmy. "Wee Men Win Big Golf Dough." *Kokomo Daily Tribune.* Indiana. April 18, 1927. p. 11.

Rice, Grantland. "Tales of a Wayside Tee." *Ogden Standard Examiner.* Ogden, Utah. March 20, 1927. p. 21.

Rogers, Will. "What America Needs Is Better Putters." *The Charleston Daily Mail.* McNaught Syndicate, Inc. January 24, 1926. p. 27.

Sinclair, Frank. "Walker Steps from Wrecked Plane and Equals Record." *Janesville Daily Gazette.* Janesville, Wisconsin. July 28, 1924. p. 10.

Smith, Horton. "Horton Says Wives Are Help to Four Professional Stars." *Joplin News Herald.* Joplin, Missouri. September 11, 1929. p. 6.

Sullivan, Ed. "Ed Sullivan's Sports Whirl." *Bakersfield Morning Echo.* Bakersfield, California. January 26, 1927. p. 5.

Unattributed Editorial. "Alibis." *Joplin News Herald.* Joplin, Missouri. January 21, 1926. p. 4.

Unattributed. "Big Golf Match at Kebo Saturday." *Bar Harbor Times.* Bar Harbor, Maine. August 15, 1923. p. 1.

Unattributed. "Braw Golfer's Wife Is Keen Bonnie Fan." *Gastonia Daily Gazette.* Gastonia, North Carolina. April 16, 1927. p. 2.

Unattributed. "Cruickshank and McLean Win at Golf." *Brewster Standard.* Brewster, New York. August 31, 1923. p. 2.

Unattributed. "Cruickshank Golf Champion Will Give Lessons to Piqua Fans." *Piqua Daily Call.* Piqua, Ohio. May 9, 1927. p. 6.

Unattributed. "Golf Title Is Captured by New Yorker." *Santa Ana Daily Register.* Santa Ana, California. August 16, 1924. p. 13.

Unattributed. "Hooks and Slides (Winter Money Winners)." *Kokomo Tribune.* Kokomo, Indiana. April 30, 1928. p. 17.

Unattributed. "Hutchinson, Evans Beat Walker and Cruickshank." *Charleston Daily Mail.* Charleston, West Virginia. July 28, 1924. p. 8.

Unattributed. "The Long Hike." *Butte Montana Standard.* Butte, Montana. November 26, 1930. p. 14.

Unattributed. "Made Big Winning on Bobby Jones." *Sedalia Capital.* Sedalia, Missouri. July 15, 1930. p. 16.

Unattributed. "Millionaire Sportsman's Hobby Brings European Golfers to US." *Salt Lake Telegram.* Salt Lake City, Utah. December 28, 1925. p. 4.

Unattributed. "The Yea and Thou Shalt Not, of a Gallery Following Play." *Galveston Daily News.* Galveston, Texas. April 3, 1923. p. 7.

United Press International. "Golfers Back from Orient." *Santa Ana Register.* Santa Ana, California. February 19, 1931. p. 8.

United Press International. "Manero Wins $1000." The *Bakersfield Californian*. Bakersfield, California. September 17, 1930. p. 14.

United Press International. "Need of Funds Has Driven Pro Golfers into Stern Training for Tournament Play." *Syracuse Herald*. Syracuse, New York. August 4, 1932. p. 52.

United Press International. "Revolta Beaten in Orlando Meet." *Charleston Gazette,* Charleston, West Virginia. December 9, 1935. p. 6.

Williams, Joe. "Golfer Rode to World Fame on Single Wallop." *Alton Evening Telegraph*. Alton, Illinois. February 19, 1924. p. 6.

Williams, Joe. "The Nut Cracker." *Alton Evening Telegraph*. Alton, Illinois. August 1, 1930. p. 10.

About the Author

Diana Smith spent countless hours on the golf course with her grandfather, Bobby Cruikshank. Learning from him gave her a unique education, both in golf and in life. She had the opportunity to play in fourteen USGA national championships: juniors, women's amateurs, and women's opens. A former teacher, she lives in the mountains of North Georgia with her husband, Joel, nine rescue dogs, and three rescue cats. Her children's poems and stories have been in magazines in the United States, Australia, and Ireland.

She loves golf because it is a game where the player is responsible for doing the right thing without someone else watching. Her golfing heritage is one of the joys of her life, and she still lives by Bobby's rules.